IMPACT

COLENSO

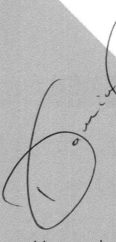

How to be more **confident**, increase your **influence** and know what to say **under pressure**

FOREWORD BY
DANIEL PRIESTLEY

R3THINK PRESS

First published in Great Britain in 2019 by Rethink Press
(www.rethinkpress.com)

© Copyright Dominic Colenso

Printed by CPI Group (UK) Ltd, Croydon CR0 4YY

Praise

'For anyone wanting to improve the way that they communicate, *IMPACT* is a must read. Dominic has engaged our finance team several times on his methodology and he really knows his stuff – he makes it fun and simple to understand. This book distils his knowledge into a practical guide that will help you get better results with any audience.'

— **Mark Laine-Toner**
   Head of Strategic Finance, Coop Food

'A terrific read with a bucketload of easy-to-implement takeaways to help anyone communicate more effectively. In this comprehensive book Dominic shares how to build influence, hone our message and create *IMPACT*.'

— **Warren Cass**
   International Speaker and Bestselling Author
   of *Influence*

'Dominic is always my go-to person when I'm looking for communication skills training for our teams. The feedback from the delegates is always fantastic and their performance is always transformed. Reading *IMPACT* is like having Dominic as your personal coach. If you want practical tools for developing more gravitas and increasing your influence in any situation, read this book. I wish I had access to it earlier in my career!'

— **Nick Walker**
   Chief Human Resources Officer, Paysafe Group

'IMPACT provides an intelligent, concise and comprehensive companion for anyone wanting to improve their communication skills. All the essential ingredients are inside, whether you are giving a business presentation, interacting in meetings or even giving a speech at a wedding! Drawn from his expertise in the worlds of acting and business, Dominic opens up a way of being in the body and the mind that builds confidence and clarity for the whole human being. Crystal clear instructions and more accessible than any other book on the topic of impact that I have read.'

— Claire Dale
Author of *Physical Intelligence*
Founder of Companies in Motion and Tutor for RADA Business

'In a world full of distractions and shiny objects it's easy to overlook the importance of mastering the fundamentals. Communication is a fundamental. Dominic knows how to help you master it. If you want to learn how to sell yourself, your ideas, your products or services I suggest making time to read and implement what he has to say. You won't regret the investment.'

— Matthew Kimberley
International Speaker, Author and Coach on the subjects of sales and persuasion

'"Training to be an actor is like training to be a musician – except that your instrument is you." Words from me to students in my sixteen years as a director at the Royal Academy of Dramatic Art. In this book Dominic Colenso, a trained, successful actor and director – and also now a sought-after business trainer – points out to those looking to boost their communication skills: "The good news is you have everything you need already." The book unpicks the simple but often elusive process of gaining and holding an audience's attention – and in business your clients and colleagues are your audience. If you're starting a start-up, or seek new, surprising energy for an established enterprise, grab this book and keep it by your bedside!'

— **Ellis Jones**
   Former Vice Principal and Head of Acting,
   Royal Academy of Dramatic Art

'Wow. Dominic Colenso has managed to do something very special: he has captured the magic and mystery of excellence in communication and laid it out in such a series of clear and practical steps that anyone reading this book, and putting the steps into practice, cannot help but increase their confidence, develop greater connection with others and become a key influencer. This book unlocks so many tacit secrets and turns them into tangible and accessible tools that everyone can immediately benefit from. If you want to increase your *IMPACT*, personally or professionally, this book is what you have been looking for!'

— **Steve Payne**
   International Executive Coach,
   Author and Keynote Speaker
   Certified Master Trainer of NLP

'A terrific guide to developing better communication skills, of interest to anyone needing to engage an audience. It's accessible, entertaining and beautifully structured. Colenso brings his experience as an actor to the art of effective communication and puts key acting techniques to excellent use.'

— **Professor Vladimir Mirodan FRSA**
   Former Principal, Drama Centre London
   Emeritus Professor of Theatre, University of the Arts London

'*IMPACT* is a roadmap for becoming an exceptional communicator. Simple to understand and easy to implement, the tools and techniques Dominic shares will help transform the way you interact with others. Whether you want to develop a winning pitch, have more influence or tell better stories, this book will help you achieve your goal.'

— **Zoe Taylor**
   Chief Operating Officer, Redington

'A great read with some real "aha" moments. Dominic uses everything he knows from the acting world to take you from simply informing to transforming people.'

— **John Williams**
   Bestselling author of *Screw Work Let's Play* and *Screw Work Break Free* Founder of The Ideas Lab

'I always tell my TEDx speakers that if they want to deliver a memorable talk, the most important thing they need to do is create an atmosphere that will propagate the connection of their unique idea in the minds of the people in the audience. If we think about it carefully, *this* is what communication is about. *This* is also what this book is about. *IMPACT* covers all the moments that lead a speaker to the creation of this special bond. If we want others to spread our ideas, we must read *IMPACT* first.'

— **Cristina Juesas**
   TEDxVitoriaGasteiz Licensee, Curator and Host
   Public Speaking Coach

'If you want to improve the way that you communicate, you couldn't ask for a better guide. This book pulls back the curtain and reveals how small changes to your behaviour can yield big results. It provides practical, sensible advice for making a stronger impression in any situation. By the time you have finished it you will have all the tools necessary to really make an *IMPACT*.'

— **Geoff Ramm**
   Creator and Author of *Celebrity Service* and
   OMG Marketing
   International Speaker and Former President of
   The Professional Speaking Association

*For Laura and Nell,
my reasons why.*

Contents

Chapter Six
TECHNIQUE   149

Chapter Seven
IMPACT IN ACTION   165

Foreword

Success in business requires the ability to influence. The best ideas, plans, forecasts, products and systems are for nothing if you cannot enrol others into your vision. Most of the time, you will be judged by what you say. Whether they're said in a meeting, on a stage or, more often these days, in a video, your words will either have power or they will drop to the floor and be swept to the side.

I run a global business accelerator, and between 2010 and 2018, our team interviewed over 6,000 entrepreneurs and leaders in the UK, the US, Australia and Singapore. Time and again, the Key People of Influence, those who were most well known and respected in their fields, were those who knew how to communicate their value. They were able to position themselves and their ideas with clarity and authority.

Verbally communicating ideas is so vitally important that the first skill we train entrepreneurs in is pitching.

Whether you're an employee, executive or business owner, working in sales or working in IT, you get what you pitch for, and you're always pitching. Numerous times a day, you're sharing your ideas and attempting to get others to buy into them. The more impactful you are in the way that you communicate, the more influence you have. Yet many people fail to make a strong impression. Their nerves get the better of them, they don't connect with their audience and their words fall flat.

Great communication runs throughout every step of building a business – from getting a first sale to raising money from investors and leading a team that can scale an enterprise. The great thing is these skills can be learned.

I first met Dominic Colenso in 2015. We were both speaking at an event in London, and when he walked onto the podium, it was clear that he had all 500 audience members in the palm of his hand. When I discovered his background as a star of stage and screen, it wasn't hard to understand why. When you're developing your skills, it's important to learn from someone with experience, someone at the top of their game. Dominic walks his talk.

What you have in your hands is a blueprint for mastering your communication – powerful bite-sized tips that will transform the way your audience perceives you and how your message lands. Dominic shares the secrets of the world's best speakers and actors in a simple and engaging way, skilfully coaching you to make the tools your own. The real value, however, is in understanding how all six ingredients of his IMPACT model come together to transform your performance. It's a step-by-step process for increasing your self-confidence and finding your voice in any situation.

No matter where you are in your career or business, this book will change the way that you communicate and will improve your results. I wish you every success on the journey and encourage you to use the tools you're about to discover to really make an impact in the world.

Daniel Priestley
Entrepreneur, best-selling author and co-founder of Dent Global
www.dent.global

Preface

I understand what it's like to feel fear and uncertainty. I've experienced the crippling effect of nerves – palms sweaty, face flushed, mouth dry; unsure of the next words to leave my mouth.

I also understand what it's like to feel the thrill of performance. I've experienced the excitement of standing in the spotlight – body relaxed, face free, breath calm; relishing the opportunity to speak.

I know which experience I enjoy the most.

I'm not a natural performer. It was a skill set that I had to learn and master, and it's now a skill set that I teach to others. For over ten years I've been working with businesses and business leaders to help people speak and perform under pressure. Through my company, In Flow, I've been lucky enough to share the information in this book with thousands of people from all sorts of organisations. But I didn't begin my career as a trainer in the training room – I began it as an actor in the theatre.

As you'll discover in the pages that follow, I was lucky enough to find success and to fulfil some of my childhood dreams. I worked on the London stage, appeared in numerous television shows and had the amazing opportunity to star in a Hollywood film. But my drama-school training and my time in the profession taught me more than how to act. It taught me how to flex my performance and get comfortable in the spotlight. It taught me the fundamental skills to be more me.

What I'm about to share with you isn't rocket science, but I hope it will open your eyes and transform your interactions. These principles are often overlooked and undervalued. The truth is that they have the power to transform your communication and your life. I'm extremely grateful that I had the chance to learn them and extremely humbled to share them with you in this book.

Introduction

It's all about impact

You can't not communicate. You're always on. Whether you're aware of it or not, others are watching your every move, listening to your tone of voice, analysing the words you use and making snap judgements about you. The funny thing is that the people judging you probably aren't even aware they're doing it. It's an unconscious act designed by our prehistoric brain to keep us safe. We're constantly surveying our environment for friend or foe. Assessing our relative status and deciding if the person in front of us poses a threat. This is great if those judgements are positive, but if they're negative in any way, the implications can be huge. You can lose the sale, miss out on a promotion, confuse investors, annoy your colleagues or make yourself look foolish, all without knowing why.

You communicate so often that I bet you rarely stop to think about how you're coming across and what impression you're leaving behind. You're in meetings, you're on the phone, you're answering emails, you're sending instant messages, you're chatting as you walk down the corridor. What if you were more effective in those moments? What if you saw each interaction as an opportunity to become more influential? What if you had the tools to really make a difference?

Improving your ability and skill as a communicator is vital to your success, regardless of your job title or your position in your organisation. How you communicate determines how much other people trust you. How you communicate determines how much other people value your ideas. How you communicate determines how much other people are willing to pay you. If you want to fulfil your potential, you need to be more strategic about what and how you communicate.

This book is for anyone who wants to do just that. You may be in a position of leadership, wanting to have more influence. Or you may be starting out on your career path, looking for a framework to help you grow your skills. As long as you're willing to deepen your self-awareness and take action, you'll gain great value from reading the pages that follow. Wherever you are on your business journey, similar challenges exist. How do you engage others? How do you inspire them to action? How do you ensure that your words get heard?

Whether you consider yourself an outstanding speaker or a complete novice, this book will help you unlock your performance in meetings and presentations. Whether you love networking or feel sick at the thought of a room full of strangers, this book will help you become more confident in any situation. Whether you're a seasoned negotiator or dread having to make a request, this book will help you have more influence and get more of what you want.

Outstanding communication is a discipline. It's a way of being; an act of performance. Just as they are in the worlds of acting and professional sports, the margins between success and failure in the world of business are small. Tiny tweaks create a ripple effect. This book is about a holistic approach to producing what legendary cycling coach Dave Brailsford calls 'marginal gains'. It's for people who want to find more flow and move from a performance that requires continual effort to one that comes easily and gets results.

While I've written this book primarily for people in the world of business, the principles are universal. They're just as applicable in your personal life as they are in your work life. It's one of the unexpected outcomes that clients often report when working with me. Not only does the quality of their work conversations improve, but conversations at home get easier too. I encourage you to take the principles I'm about to share with you and apply them in all areas of your life. If you do, I promise that you'll reap the rewards.

The good news is you have everything you need already. You are enough. Your unique experiences and insights are a powerful combination that you can use to fuel your performance. This book isn't about transforming you into someone else. It's about equipping you with the tools to choose which sides of your personality you reveal. It's about empowering you to make an impact.

The IMPACT model

A great performance requires certain ingredients. If one (or more) of these is missing, the impact for the audience is diminished. You can say the right words but for some reason your message doesn't land. Conversely, you can appear confident and in control but no one acts on your words because your message isn't clear. Your communication is complex, and you need all the elements to come together in just the right way to achieve peak performance.

Having observed what works and what doesn't for some of the top performers in the worlds of acting and business, I've identified the six vital ingredients of effective communication. These six areas of focus form the basis of my IMPACT model. In isolation these things are important, but in combination their power is exponential. They will allow you to tap into a way of communicating that is authentic and compelling, helping you persuade others and gain traction, whatever your message. When all six ingredients are present, your communication will flow easily and other people will pay attention to what you say. Let's look at each of them in turn.

THE IMPACT MODEL

I   INTENTION

M   MINDSET

P   PRESENCE

A   AUDIENCE

C   CONTENT

T   TECHNIQUE

Intention

Define what you want and ensure that you get it.

When people think about an intention or objective, they tend to intellectualise it: 'What do I want my audience to understand? What are the key messages I want to get across?' These are useful questions, but they're only part of the picture. You need to remember that you're talking to multifaceted human beings, so it's vital to take a multifaceted approach. Of course you need to think about what you want your audience to know; what information you need to get across. But to be really effective, you also need to pay attention to what you want them to feel. You need to engage people on an emotional level as well as an intellectual one. You must engage hearts as well as minds. Finally, to measure your success, you need to be clear on what action you want people to take. What do you want them to do? When you can articulate a three-pronged intention, you set yourself up for success.

Mindset

Control the voices in your head.

We all have an inner voice. We're constantly evaluating our own performance, and most of the time we're our own harshest critic. Rather than being encouraging and acting as a cheerleader, often we talk ourselves down and put up barriers. How many times have you told yourself that other people disagree with what you're saying or are finding your contribution boring, only to discover later that your fears were unfounded? Controlling, or at least taming, your self-talk helps you to feel and appear more confident. If you want to make an impact and influence others, you first need to influence yourself and ensure that you're approaching your performance with the right mindset. It's about more than just having a positive mental attitude – it's about directing your thoughts so that they serve your intentions.

Presence

Harness the power of your body and your voice.

As we've already established, whether you like it or not, people are constantly reading into the signals you send out through your body and your voice. They're using this information to decide how much they trust you and whether they'll listen to your words. However, your physical and vocal presence doesn't just affect others; it also plays a big part in your own feelings of confidence and power. Actors become sensitive to how changes in the way they use their bodies alter their emotional state and that of their audience. The same is true in the world of business. Simple adjustments to the way you stand, sit and speak can have a massive impact on how your words are received. We all have habitual ways of using our instrument of communication, but the body is incredibly adaptable; with some conscious effort, you'll quickly develop a more impactful presence.

Audience

Understand who's listening and speak their language.

We all have our own way of doing things, and so does our audience. If we're closely aligned with the people we're speaking to, the communication is usually easy. But if we lack that connection, it can feel like we're speaking completely different languages. Conflict and misunderstanding usually arise when you haven't taken time to understand the other party's point of view. The more adept you are at stepping into your audience's shoes, the more effective your communication will be. From a place of understanding, you can flex your style for maximum impact. You don't have to agree with the opposite point of view, but you do need to hear it if you are to successfully lead the conversation. To help you do this, I've created a powerful model to enable you to identify other people's preferences and unlock your own communication. Combine this with sharpened listening skills and you can develop the ability to instantly read a room and deliver a more focused and influential message.

Content

Choose your words to create maximum engagement.

Sometimes finding the right words feels impossible. When you're starting a presentation, delivering one-to-one feedback or speaking up in the heat of a meeting, deciding what to say in order to have the right effect can be difficult. You need to choose your words wisely. However, over-planning can lead you to sound scripted and inauthentic. Your audience will quickly stop listening if they don't believe what you're saying or can't relate to your message. If you know your topic inside out, there is a danger that you'll get lost in the detail and fail to bring your content to life in the hearts and minds of your audience. Simple structures are the key to creating more impact, allowing you to be flexible with your words but deliberate in your message. With the right foundations in place, you can start painting pictures with your language to capture your listeners' imaginations.

Technique

Make your performance consistent and authentic.

You are unique. As a communicator, that's part of your strength. The objective of this book isn't to churn out cookie-cutter clones who all speak and interact in the same way. I want to help you amplify your impact and showcase your strengths. To do this, you need to make the tools your own and apply them to your own situation. Just as each actor who has ever tackled the role of Hamlet has brought their own experience to the part, so too will you bring your own experience to your performance.

But underpinning that performance is your technique. Just like a great actor, you must develop the muscles of communication. The tools I'm about to share need to be practised in context if they are to look and feel authentic. They need to move from intellectual concept to muscle memory. Put in the work and they will quickly become your own.

The order is important

If you want to increase your impact, you need to take the process step by step. It's tempting to skip straight into the spotlight and focus on your performance, but if the building blocks aren't in place, the whole thing will come tumbling down. You have to approach your communication systematically. These six ingredients build logically upon one another. It doesn't matter how commanding your presence is if you don't have a clear intention. You can work on your technique all day long but if you don't have the right mindset, you're setting yourself up to fail. Your beautifully crafted content will count for nothing if you fail to understand your audience. If you want to create an impact, you need to address each element in sequence. It might take some time to ensure each building block is in place, but soon using the IMPACT model will become instinctive. Once you've set your intention, you can focus your mindset, ensure you are present, consider your audience, plan your content and unleash your technique – all in a matter of seconds. It's what we instinctively do in day-to-day life. My job is to bring your attention to each step of the process to ensure that you create maximum impact.

I've seen many people transform themselves using the ideas and methods I'm going to share with you. They've grown in confidence, re-energised their teams, guided their organisations through times of change and positioned themselves as experts in their industries. I've also seen some try to rush straight to the end result and fail. Making an impact takes effort. If you want to reach the top of your game, you'll need to put in the work. My aim is to be your guide. To challenge your current thinking. To hold your hand when necessary and to open your eyes to your potential. I'm going to share the communications toolkit that I've developed as an actor and a coach, and I invite you to explore which tools work best for you. My final objective is to propel you into action.

Acts of communication

The tips and tricks we'll work through together are not things to be filed away in the back of your mind for use in the distant future. They are things I want you to experiment with right away. One of the most valuable lessons I learned as an actor was the power of improvisation. In life we tend to wait for a 'safe space', a moment when no one is looking before we dare to experience and experiment. If you adopted that approach as an actor, you would never create anything. I want you to think of our time together as you read this book as 'rehearsal time'. An opportunity to try some things on for size, to experiment, to dare to fail and to push yourself in new directions.

You'll find numerous 'acts of communication' scattered throughout the text to help you do this – exercises that can be completed immediately and that will deepen your understanding and experience. Of course, you'll still get value from reading these pages without doing them, but if you want to create an impact, I promise it will be worth the effort.

Look out for the video ▶ and download ⬇ icons throughout the book for links to additional resources.

Chapter One

INTENTION

Know what you want

Throughout my training and subsequent work as an actor, one question dominated the rehearsal room. Whether I was interrogating a stage play or a film script, playing a hero or a villain, or working on a tragedy or a comedy, the first question the director would always ask was 'What do you want?' Not 'What do you want?' personally, from the point of view of the actor, but from the point of view of the character in the scene. What was the character trying to achieve? What was driving them to act? At every moment of my performance I needed to be able to understand and articulate my character's motivation. Why was the character doing what they were doing?

I was lucky enough to attend one of the best drama schools in the UK, renowned for turning out talented and transformational actors such as Tom Hardy, Gwendoline Christie, Colin Firth, Michael Fassbender and Helen McCrory. It was also renowned for its rigorous methodology. I vividly remember sitting in acting classes in my first few weeks wondering why they were being so pedantic about the way we articulated our objective. Surely it wasn't that important. How would the audience know if we had done it or not? What difference would it make? Then, one wet November afternoon, the penny dropped. We were in rehearsals for a Chekhov play and I was working on a pivotal line. It seemed like a simple sentence, but every time I opened my mouth it somehow didn't sound right. The words came out flat. We went around and around in circles for what seemed like an age. 'What do you want?' the director kept asking, but I struggled to come up with a decent answer. It took half an hour for me to discover the right intention, but when I did, all of a sudden, the words sang. From that moment on, 'What do you want?' became my starting point – the question I answered before I did anything else.

It might sound like common sense, but this same question should be your starting point for effective communication in business. 'What do I want?' 'What is my objective in this situation?' 'What am I looking to achieve right now?' The problem with common sense is that it's not that common. A lot of people 'wing it'. The higher you rise in an organisation, the more demands there are on your time. And the more demands there are on your time, the easier it is to forget to set aside time to plan. So many people move from one overrunning meeting to the next, desperately trying to catch up, without making time to set clear goals for their interactions. The energy from Meeting A seeps into Meeting B, so if Meeting A goes badly, Meeting B will pick up the same tone and you won't really know why.

If you want to drive the narrative and increase your influence, you have to know what you're trying to achieve before you take the first steps. In the world of acting, we call this knowing your intention. It's a process that allows you to quickly and efficiently bring your objective to life, making it 'playable' so that others can act upon it. To create maximum impact, I suggest thinking about your intention as having three distinct parts.

Unlock the power of three

As an actor, asking the question 'What do I want?' leads you to an overarching objective: 'I want to make the girl fall in love with me' or 'I want to steal the money without anyone noticing'. It's a useful starting point, but on its own, an objective like this is too big to play. It's too generalised. To be really effective, it needs to be broken down into smaller parts.

The same is true in business. In the unlikely event that we've stopped to consider our reason for attending a meeting or picking up the phone, we've normally done so only at a macro level – 'I want to update the team on the status of the project' or 'I want to get the client to agree to the purchase'. This level of thinking is too simplistic. Just like the actor in the rehearsal room, you need to dig deeper. You need to ask some additional questions.

Often, we think at a purely intellectual or logical level and concern ourselves with information exchange. We ask, 'What do I want the audience to know?' or, 'What information do I need to convey in this situation?' To have more impact, you must go further and consider what you want your audience to feel and do as well.

What do you want your audience to…

- Know?

- Feel?

- Do?

This powerful combination of three questions allows you to move your communication from the transactional to the transformational. You start to be able to take your audience on a journey and ensure that they're in a different place, mentally and emotionally, after their interactions with you. Let's explore each of these three parts in more detail.

Know: your intellectual intention

Your 'intellectual intention' is what you want your audience to know. This might seem obvious, but to maximise your chances of success, you need to get specific. Often when we communicate something we do so from the position of the 'expert'. That doesn't mean we're the world's leading authority on a subject; it just means that we're the person in the room with the most information on it. You may not realise it, but most of the time, if you're asked to speak on a topic or invited to a meeting, it's because others feel you can add value with your knowledge. The challenge lies in the fact that we're normally unaware of just how much we know. If you've been in a role for more than a few months, you will have amassed a body of expertise in a niche. Whether that niche is 'bio-concrete application in the construction industry' or 'the stationery requirements of the Edinburgh office', you have a wealth of information at your fingertips. The trick is making it interesting, relevant and memorable for your audience. When you achieve this combination, your message becomes 'sticky' – people find it easy to retain what you have said.

Keep it simple

To construct this 'sticky' message, you must filter what needs to be said from what could be said. What is the essential, core message? When we're knowledgeable or passionate about a subject, we tend to want to tell people everything we know. The problem with this is that it's overwhelming. On any given day we have thousands of messages competing for our attention – advertisements, social media, news, emails, meetings, phone calls – so, if a message isn't simple to grasp, it's easier for our brains to delete it than to go through the effort of deciphering it. This means we need to think strategically about what we say. What are the key takeaways for the audience? If they could remember only three things, what should they be?

When it comes to the language you use, keep things simple. There's a reason that tabloid newspapers sell more copies than broadsheets. Whether you agree with them or not, their messages are constructed in a way that makes it easy for everyone to understand their position. They don't get caught up in jargon or complex language, and they set out their core message in the simplest way possible. Tabloid headlines are rarely longer than seven words, and most of these words will consist of seven letters or fewer. Think like a tabloid editor and simplify your message. How could you make things more memorable for your audience?

One thing I see clients struggling with is making their core message succinct. We often try to get lots of things across in a single interaction. But for the most part, this dilutes our impact and confuses our audience. In communication, less really is more. We don't want to leave people feeling overwhelmed – we want to give them clarity and certainty. Think about your core message as a concentrated version of your idea. If you had to boil down everything you wanted to say into as few words as possible, what would those words be? Remember that audiences aren't great at retaining information, so don't overload them. If you're speaking for five minutes or less, a single message is all you have time for. As a rule of thumb, if I had five to thirty minutes I'd be focusing on a maximum of three points, and if I had sixty minutes, I'd be working with six key ideas but no more. Here's the acid test: Ask your audience what they've taken away from what you've just said. If they can repeat your core message, you know that you've made an impact.

The information you want people to know needs to pass what I call the five-year-old test. If you can't explain your idea to a five-year-old child in a way that they can understand, you're overcomplicating things. It's important to note that I'm not suggesting you should dumb down your content or oversimplify. When explaining concepts and ideas, you may have to use nuanced terminology and vocabulary, but your key messages, the things you need people to remember, must be as simple as possible. For example, the scientific basis for gravity is incredibly intricate but the idea that 'what goes up must come down' is easy to understand.

Beware of jargon and acronyms too. It's easy to fall into the trap of assuming everyone understands the terminology that you take for granted. Even when you're communicating internally in your organisation, it's best to assume that people have no prior knowledge of what you're talking about. People switch off when they hear acronym-laden sentences because they sound robotic and have limited resonance. You also run the risk of isolating those who aren't familiar with the concepts, or at least losing their attention while they try to process what your random combination of three letters means!

ACT OF COMMUNICATION

● ●

WRITE THE HEADLINE

A useful way to get clear on your intellectual intention is to write the newspaper headline and subheadings for the message you want to convey. Ask yourself what big idea you want your audience to hear. This becomes your headline. Then create three subheadings – three key bits of information that you want your audience to remember. Here are a couple of examples:

HEADLINE:
   Sales Targets Smashed By 12%
SUBHEADINGS:
   1. Five new clients won
   2. Average order value doubled
   3. New marketing campaign producing warmer leads

HEADLINE:
   New IT System Boosts Productivity
SUBHEADINGS:
   1. Real-time telephone support available
   2. Software streamlined across the company
   3. Data stored securely

This process will help you get clear on your messaging and get you used to choosing language that's easy for your audience to understand.

● ●

Say it often

Once you've defined exactly what it is you want people to know, you must be prepared to keep repeating it. The rule of seven is an old marketing concept that suggests that people need to see, hear or experience your message seven times before they buy. In today's world of information overload, I suspect that number is even higher. As we sit at our computers, multiple platforms compete for our attention. Our inboxes ping. Notifications ding. Adverts and clickbait crowd our browsers. If we want our message to land, we have to rise above the noise and repeat it often. You need to signpost to your audience the important information that you want them to take away. You don't need to make it as obvious as retargeted Google Ads, but you do need to make sure your audience is in no doubt about what you want them to hear. The importance of repetition applies to all formats and forums. Whether you're writing a sales document or an email, giving a presentation or having an informal chat, speaking with a large audience or meeting one-to-one, you need to keep highlighting your key messages. The better you are at defining and repeating them, the greater the chances that they'll land. Keep it simple. Keep it simple. Keep it simple.

Feel: your emotional intention

The next part of the intention jigsaw is thinking about how you want to make your audience feel. Humans are emotionally intuitive beings. We use our emotions to make sense of the world. Our feelings influence our decisions and our motivations. Therefore, it's the job of a great communicator to take their audience on an emotional journey, to make them feel something. We want them to be different at the end of the interaction than they were at the beginning. Any good film or piece of theatre provides those watching with some form of catharsis. The audience is invited to share the emotional experience of the characters they're watching. That shared experience is something humans have craved since we first huddled round the fires in our caves telling stories, and it's just as relevant now as it was thousands of years ago.

We continually engage with our emotions in our personal lives, but in the workplace, they can get switched off. There's often some stigma attached to emotions in the world of work – showing emotion or being emotional could be seen as a weakness. In fact, the opposite is true. The more you're able to make your audience feel, the greater your influence. Thankfully, as the concept of 'emotional intelligence' becomes more widespread, attitudes are beginning to change and people are starting to understand the power of creating a connection at this level. The benefits of engaging our audience emotionally are huge. If people are emotionally invested in what we're saying, we can create deeper commitment and accountability, and our ideas are much more likely to resonate. So how do you ensure that you create the right emotional reaction? This is where the concept of 'emotional intention' comes into play.

Are you talking to me?

Humans are adaptable. We have objectives and we try lots of different tactics to get what we desire. We'll continue to change tactics until we get what we want or, worst-case scenario, we'll give up and reassess our objective. I call these tactics emotional intentions. Our emotional intentions are what we want the people we're interacting with to feel; the emotional journey we want to take them on. We can say the same phrase with a different emotional intention and the meaning for the audience changes. Emotional intention was a cornerstone of my drama-school training, and the technique is used widely by actors to help them create interesting and varied performances. A great example of this is the scene in one of my favourite films, *Taxi Driver*, where Robert De Niro stands in front of the mirror saying, 'Are you talking to me?' over and over. Each time he speaks the words, the intention changes and so does the impact. If you've never seen it, make sure you check it out. It's a masterclass!

When we're defining an emotional intention, we use transitive verbs – 'doing' words that create an emotional reaction. I may feel passionate about my subject matter, but if I want other people to feel passionate about it too, I have to do something to them. I might want to excite, energise or even motivate. Most people make the mistake that bad actors make. They focus on their own emotion rather than trying to move their audience. This is ultimately an act of self-indulgence. You can be as passionate as you like but unless you actively try to change your audience, your emotion will have little impact.

You need to clarify your emotional intention before every interaction. What do you want people to feel? When you're able to identify this, it influences the way that your words sound. The tone, pace, pitch, volume and speed are all instinctively different depending on the emotional intention that you decide to convey. When you change what you're trying to do to your audience, it changes the way that the words come out of your mouth. The great thing about transitive verbs is that there are thousands of them. This means that you can continually vary your message to suit the situation.

Below is a list of active verbs to help stimulate your thinking about emotional intentions. These are just examples. There are thousands of verbs in the dictionary, so pick the ones that resonate with you personally. To make sure you're using a verb and not an emotional state, simply insert the word into this sentence: 'Can my audience feel (verb) ed?' If the answer is YES, you're on the right track!

EMOTIONAL INTENTIONS

Alarm	Congratulate	Frighten	Restrain
Align	Convert	Harness	Rouse
Animate	Convince	Ignite	Scare
Applaud	Dare	Implore	Seduce
Approve	Delight	Impress	Sell
Assure	Dissuade	Influence	Shame
Awaken	Dominate	Inspire	Shock
Boost	Educate	Instruct	Stimulate
Brighten	Encourage	Intrigue	Surprise
Calm	Energise	Involve	Teach
Caution	Entertain	Motivate	Tempt
Celebrate	Enthuse	Persuade	Threaten
Challenge	Entice	Praise	Touch
Charm	Excite	Protect	Unite
Coach	Fascinate	Provoke	Uplift
Comfort	Flatter	Reassure	Value
Compliment	Focus	Reprimand	Warn

To download a free copy of the Emotional Intentions worksheet visit www.inflow.global/resources

Let's look at how you might use this in a business context. Imagine your team have been underperforming. You need to communicate to them that the progress so far on a project has been unacceptable. You have a new process that you'd like them to implement to improve results and have set some ambitious targets that you want them to achieve in the coming weeks. In a meeting setting, this sort of message could easily cause resentment, frustration or disengagement in the team. However, change the intention and you'll change how your words land. Deliver the bad news as a challenge, educate the team on your new process and inspire them with the targets you've set. All of a sudden, you've taken them on a journey – they'll receive the information in a very different way.

ACT OF COMMUNICATION

CHANGE THE EMOTION

Getting clear on your emotional intention will change how your words come out of your mouth. Say this out loud: 'Good morning, everyone. We've got lots to talk about today.' Now imagine that your intention is to challenge the audience. Speak the same words with this new intention. Notice how the sound automatically changes. Now try to excite the audience. The words are the same but somehow they have different meaning. This is the power of intention. When you know what emotional impact you want to have on your audience, your performance takes care of itself.

Plan the journey

Another benefit of deciding your emotional intentions in advance is that you can use them as a roadmap.
Think of it like changing gear while driving. You need
to select the appropriate gear for the terrain you find
yourself on. Try going uphill in fifth gear and you'll
quickly find yourself in trouble. Match your intention
to the situation and it smooths your communication.
It also helps you choose the most appropriate content
and language.

I regularly use emotional intentions as a framework
for planning meetings and presentations. How do I
want people to feel? What's the journey I want to take
them on? What are the different steps – the beginning,
the middle and the end? Three distinct and compelling
emotional intentions can give you enough stimulus
for a ten-minute talk without any notes. Trust that you
know your area of expertise and then commit to how
you want the audience to feel. It's a great technique,
especially when you have little or no time to prepare
and need to speak off the cuff. It's the sort of thing you
can literally plan on the back of a napkin.

Anywhere in the ballpark will do

The other thing I love about this technique is the fact
that it's secret. You don't have to make your emotional
intentions explicit. In fact, it's probably best not to.

Most people don't like being told how to feel, so this relieves you of the pressure of getting it 'right'. It's unlikely that someone is going to come up to you after a meeting, pat you on the back and name the emotional intention you were playing. Instead, if you've done your job, you'll have triggered an emotional response. You might have been trying to 'inspire', and they may feel 'motivated', 'energised' or 'engaged'. All these things are in the same ballpark. They have similar emotional qualities. What's important is that those in the meeting are unlikely to feel 'threatened' or 'reprimanded'. They may not be able to name the emotion exactly, but they'll normally be close.

Stop informing

The one word I want you to ban from your lexicon of emotional intentions is 'inform'. As far as I'm aware, no one has ever, in the history of meetings and presentations, walked out of an office grinning from ear to ear and uttered, 'That was great. I feel so informed!' Don't get me wrong. We're always transmitting information to our audience. That's an absolute given. But if we want to make an impact, we have to move beyond the transactional and pursue the transformational. When we can communicate effectively, we can convey information in myriad ways to engage the audience's hearts as well as their minds. If your intention is simply to 'inform', consider sending an email so that your content can be consumed on your audience's own terms; don't take up their time face-to-face or on the phone.

As a footnote to this section, it's worth mentioning the concept of updates. I've worked with numerous organisations and teams that hold monthly, weekly and sometimes even daily update sessions. We should be updating software not humans. Don't just think about information exchange – think about the emotional tone you want to create. What are you really trying to do when you give an update? What response are you looking for from the audience? Think about how, not just what, you deliver.

Do: your behavioural intention

The final element of intention is your 'behavioural intention'. What do you want people to do? What action do you want them to take? Communication is an active process. It's a transfer of energy from the communicator to the audience. When we communicate effectively, this transfer of energy creates movement and momentum in our listeners. The word 'act' is built into the word 'impact' – we should measure our impact through the actions of others. Have we changed behaviour? Have we been able to create movement? To measure your success, you need to define your outcome in advance. Once you know what you want people to do, you can assess whether your communication has moved them to do it.

Give a call to action

Always finish important interactions with a call to action. It should be the thing that's ringing in your audience's ears as they leave. Your call to action is your behavioural intention in its most concentrated form, and it needs to be explicit. Many people are guilty of expecting their audiences to be mind readers. They hint at what they want but don't actually ask for it. Directness is vital in a sales context – you always have to ask for the sale – but it's relevant in all communication. When someone finishes reading the email you sent, or puts down the phone after a conversation with you, do they know exactly what your expectations are and have they been agreed? If you ever played the 'telephone game' as a child, you'll know how quickly and easily meaning can get distorted or lost, so it's important that you get comfortable with making your call to action explicit rather than trying to hide it. Whether you're communicating through the written or the spoken word, it's a good idea to state it at least twice, first near the beginning and second right at the end. This maximises the chances of your call to action landing. Your audience will know what you want early on, and this message will also be the thing you leave them thinking about.

Make the steps small

Most people have a lot on their plates. We live busy lives and can feel overwhelmed by the sheer volume of things on our to-do lists. So if you want to maximise your impact, it's useful to have an awareness of this to ensure that your requests don't end up on other people's 'someday/maybe' list. Instead of painting the big picture and leaving your audience to figure out their part in it, get prescriptive. Doing so will pay dividends. The more you can break things down into small steps, the less resistance and fear you'll trigger in others. 'Write a 250-word introduction' is much less scary and much easier to do than 'Start writing a progress report for the board'. Paint a picture of the overall outcome or direction and then show others the roadmap for how to get there, so that it feels achievable. The more specific you are about the steps you want them to take, the more likely they are to take them. Most of us know this in theory but fail to put it into practice. Your being able to share small steps proves to your audience that you've thought through your argument and have put yourself in their shoes. This attention to detail allows you to focus your audience's minds and energy and will ultimately lead to a much better outcome.

Stay positive when articulating your behavioural intention, it's useful to think about the words you use. The neuroscience around the use of positive language is a little hazy. Some research suggests that in certain circumstances, the brain has difficulty processing instructions stated in the negative; other studies rubbish the claim. Rather than wade into the debate, let's look at it anecdotally, from a more personal perspective. Would you rather listen to a list of things you can do, or a list of things you can't? Would you rather be asked to do something politely, or threatened into action? I don't know about you, but I'd rather be talked to nicely. Humans have a natural negative bias. We've been designed to look for danger and to do what we can to keep ourselves safe. It's easy to follow this negative bias and fall into the trap of positioning your behavioural intention in negative terms. Instead, challenge yourself to restate it in the positive. If you want to build trust and engagement, remember that you're much more likely to galvanise people around a positive message. I'm not saying don't ever use negatives. There are times when it's useful to get people to focus on what to avoid, but if we always go in that direction, the impact gets watered down. So, as a general rule, stay away from the dark side and step towards the light.

ACT OF COMMUNICATION

• •

MEASURE YOUR SUCCESS

Before your next meeting, presentation or phone call, take five minutes to plan your behavioural intention. Don't just do it in your head. Write it down. Grab a blank piece of paper and write the word 'DO' in the middle. Then fill the page with descriptions of the evidence of your success. It could be the body language of your audience – getting a smile or a nod. It could be what other people say in response – a yes or an agreement to consider things further. Or it could be something more tangible – a signed contract or a new job title. What would success look like, sound like and feel like? Once you've defined the evidence of the success you're looking for, it becomes much easier to measure your performance. After the interaction, take a moment to review your outcome. Did you get the things you wrote down? Did your behavioural intention land? Use the acronym WWWEBI to prompt your reflection: What went well? Even better if?

• •

Take thirty seconds

Getting clear on your intentions can seem like an overwhelming task. In reality, you can do it incredibly quickly. It needn't be something you agonise over, and the more you practise, the easier it will become. Get into the habit of taking thirty seconds before every interaction you have to ask yourself the three questions I posed earlier:

What do you want your audience to…

- Know?

- Feel?

- Do?

Knowing your intellectual, emotional and behavioural intention is the foundation of effective communication. It's what you build the rest of your performance on. Get used to making time to explore all three and you'll quickly see your impact transform.

Chapter Two

MINDSET

It's all in your head

I admit it. I hear voices. And I believe everyone else does too. In fact, you're probably thinking, 'What voices is he talking about? I'm perfectly normal, thank you!' And that's exactly the sort of voice I'm referring to. We all have an internal dialogue – a running commentary of self-evaluation and self-criticism. And I use the word 'criticism' deliberately. For some reason, our voices are never entirely positive. Most of the time, they're pointing out what could go or has gone wrong, focusing on the dangers in a vain attempt to keep us safe from our weaknesses. The problem is that if we allow these voices to dominate, they can completely derail our performance.

My first job as an actor was in a BBC period drama called *The Lost Prince*. I'd landed a small role playing the young King Edward VIII (Duke of Windsor), who went on to abdicate the throne and marry Wallis Simpson.

I was still in my final year of drama school, and it was a great opportunity. I was really excited but also incredibly nervous. The show was being directed by the legendary Stephen Poliakoff and the cast list included the great and the good of the British acting establishment: Tom Hollander, Bill Nighy, Miranda Richardson and Sir Michael Gambon, to name a few. My first experience of acting professionally in front of the camera was not a simple two-person dialogue or an establishing shot of me walking through the palace grounds. Instead, on my first day on set, we were shooting a big crowd scene where I would have to recite poetry in front of two hundred extras, fifty crew members and all my acting idols. I was petrified. The voices in my head were out of control.

I'd met the other cast members during costume fittings and make-up tests, and they were lovely, but as I stepped onto set to film the scene, I felt isolated. I'd learned my lines, I'd done my research, I'd rehearsed my performance. But the voices in my head weren't being supportive. 'You don't deserve to be here.' 'Don't mess this up – there are 250 people watching you!' 'Everyone's going to know this is the first time you've done this.' Not helpful. When the director shouted 'Action', time seemed to slow down, and the lines that I'd learned inside out and back to front evaporated from my head. My mouth was dry and my mind was blank. I was frozen to the spot. I finally managed to spit out the first sentence but couldn't finish the speech. To my shame, I heard the director shout 'Cut' and I was told that we were going to go for a second take. Again I stumbled, and the voices in my head got louder. The show was being shot on film and time really was money. I was feeling the pressure. The nightmare continued until all of a sudden, during my fourth disastrous attempt, something broke the pattern. Out in the audience, someone began roaring with laughter. Sir Michael Gambon (most famous for playing Dumbledore in the Harry Potter films) was playing my grandfather in the show. Seeing my discomfort and the trouble I was in, he had decided to lighten the mood. As I struggled to find my words, he rose to his feet and began to clap. In that second, he took all the focus and pressure off me, and then, in an act of generosity that I will always be grateful for, he smiled at me, winked and whispered, 'Don't worry. You'll be fine.' Those five words were all I needed. The voices in my head were silenced and I could focus on the task at hand. The next take I was word-perfect, my confidence grew and I finally began to enjoy my performance.

If we want to perform at our best, we need to take control of our internal dialogue and ensure that what we say to ourselves in those crucial moments is a help and not a hindrance. Unfortunately, we won't always have a Knight of the British Empire by our side to help us get back on track, so we need to develop replicable strategies to ensure that we master our mindset when the stakes are high.

Understand the mind-body link

We've established that we all have moments of doubt – that from time to time, we all suffer from imposter syndrome and wonder if people are really buying into what we're saying. The challenge then becomes influencing our thinking and turning self-doubt into self-belief. One of the most valuable lessons I learned as an actor is that the body can change the mind.

Freeze. Don't move a muscle. Notice how you're sitting or standing as you read these words. Now notice how you feel. Energised? Lethargic? Curious? Whatever you were doing with your body, I want you to change it. Sit up or stand up. Make yourself as big as possible. If no one else is around, have a little stretch. Yawn. Take a couple of deep breaths. Did you do it? What are you waiting for? I thought you were going to try this stuff out? Now notice how you're feeling. Any different? If you've followed my instructions, I guarantee that you're feeling more energised and awake.

The way we use our bodies deeply influences our feelings and our mindset, but most of us are unaware of our own performances in this respect. Pay attention to your body next time you're stressed and I bet you'll notice muscular tension and tightness in certain places. It might be in your shoulders. It might be in your jaw. It might even be in your buttocks. Conversely, focus on your body next time you feel relaxed and calm – there will be much more freedom and flexibility in your movement, accompanied by a reduction in muscular tension. The great thing about this is that if we can bring more attention to what we're doing physically, we can start to change how we feel. By understanding the mind-body link, we can quickly and easily start to influence our mindset. Next time you experience an unwanted emotion, observe your posture and, most importantly, change it. If you're feeling tense, shake things out. If your body is contracted, take up more space. If you're moving slowly, quicken the pace. Learn what works for you.

Actors use these changes in dynamic energy to help create a character. How would the person you're playing move? What sort of posture would they have? Of course, in real life you're not playing a character, you're just trying to be the best version of yourself, but the same principles apply. We'll look at physical presence in more detail later in the book but for now, listen to your body and pay attention to what it's telling you and your audience. Simple changes to the way you use your physicality will have a massive impact on your state of mind.

Take a deep breath

Just as our physicality impacts our thoughts and feelings, so does the way we breathe. In fact, the two things are interlinked. When your body is tense, elevated levels of the stress hormone cortisol are present in your bloodstream. To make things worse, the physical tension is likely to make you breathe in a way that increases your threat response – your unconscious 'fight-or-flight' reaction to stressful situations. If you want to take control of your mindset you must first take control of your breath. Eastern cultures have long focused on the power of our breathing to reduce stress and increase feelings of presence. For decades actors have been taught breath work as a way of both calming their nerves and fuelling their voice. Thankfully, the general population is finally catching up. We're seeing mindfulness and meditation enter the mainstream, and high-performers in the world of sport are using breathing techniques as a way of enhancing their performance too.

We were born with complete command over our breathing and vocal apparatus. Newborn babies cry at high decibels for hours on end without ever getting a sore throat. Watch a child's belly as they inhale and you'll clearly see the breath coming low into the body as they breathe from the diaphragm, abdominals relaxed, ribcage expanding as the lungs fill with air. It's how we were born to breathe. It's how we breathe when we're sleeping and when we exert ourselves physically. However, by the time we reach adulthood, most of us have made an unconscious change. Whether it's the result of a desire to have a flat stomach (or at least to suck in as much as possible) or years of sitting in a classroom being told to quieten down, most adults I work with breathe predominantly into the chest.

This shallow, thoracic breathing has two major draw-backs. It negatively affects the voice and it negatively affects the mind. Not only does this way of breathing make it difficult to effectively vocalise your thoughts and give them colour, but in high-stakes situations, it also makes you prone to feelings of unease and nervousness.

As we'll explore later, the foundation of vocal presence is diaphragmatic breathing, but it also does amazing things for quieting the mind in moments of stress. In some ways the human brain has evolved very little since the time we lived in caves, hunting and scavenging for food in order to survive. When we're under pressure, our ancient fight-or-flight response is triggered and the body does everything it can to protect us. This is great news if you happen to be being chased by a sabre-toothed tiger but not so useful if you're delivering a presentation or speaking up during an important meeting. Your body's sympathetic nervous system is activated and your bloodstream is flooded with adrenaline and the stress hormone cortisol. This results in your breathing becoming quicker and shallower, which only compounds the problem. The only thing to do in this situation is take a deep breath. This will help you to combat the reaction and bring your response under control. Anyone who has ever suffered from panic attacks will know the importance of diaphragmatic breathing in calming the mind. It's a technique we can all benefit from, and it's easy to learn.

ACT OF COMMUNICATION

· ·

BREATHE FOR SUCCESS

Find a quiet place to sit and allow your body to relax. Scan the body from the top of your head to your toes, and if you notice any tension just let it melt away. Start to focus on the breath. Soften the stomach muscles. Place one hand just below your belly button and focus on breathing low. As you breathe in, your belly will expand as the lungs fill with air. As you breathe out, your belly will contract as the air is expelled. Don't try to force things or overthink what you're doing. If the breath is short, it's short. If it's long, it's long. Since your first second on the planet, your body has been taking care of this important function. Trust that as you continue to relax, it will know what to do. Spend a couple of minutes breathing in this way and you'll notice a feeling of calm start to spread through your body and mind. There's no need to control your thoughts. Just notice them. Then let them go and return your focus to the breath. This technique is useful to practise before any important interaction and can even be deployed 'in situ' during stressful meetings and conversations.

· ·

The above technique is my go-to tool when I'm under pressure. Ten to fifteen minutes before an important event you'll always find me focusing on my breathing. I won't necessarily be sitting in a darkened room meditating, but as I go about my business, some of my attention will be on making sure that I'm breathing deeply.

It helps me clear my mind of unwanted, unhelpful thoughts and allows me to stay laser focused on the task at hand.

● ●

 To watch my video about breathing, visit www.inflow.global/breathing

● ●

Nerves vs excitement

Another useful technique to use when faced with a situation that puts you out of your comfort zone is to reframe your nerves as excitement. A little bit of adrenaline can be really useful, as it makes you alert and energised. Actors, athletes and extreme-sports junkies continually place themselves in environments that would make most of us feel nervous and uncomfortable. And yet, rather than running away from the pressure, they lean in and seem to enjoy it. This may seem like a superhuman power, but they've simply learned to change the label. Instead of saying they feel nervous, they report feelings of excitement. If you had to tell a doctor about the symptoms you were suffering from if you were nervous or excited, you would find them incredibly similar: increased heart rate, increased perspiration, pupil dilation, thinking about future events, etc. So, instead of feeling nervous next time you're under pressure, try telling yourself that you're excited. You'll be amazed by what a difference it makes.

Challenge your beliefs

Now that we've got some techniques for clearing the mind and quieting the voices, let's pause to think about what it is these voices are actually saying. Why do they tend to be negative and unhelpful rather than positive and supportive? Why do they focus on everything that's going wrong rather than everything that's going right? The answer lies in the beliefs we hold about ourselves. When you're in a state of flow, doing something you love or are skilled at, the voices in your head are silent. The minutes and hours fly by without you even noticing because you're engrossed in the task at hand. If the voices are saying anything at all, the dialogue is positive and constructive and adds to your enjoyment of the experience. Your belief in your ability to succeed and perform well at the task is high.

The problem comes when we're engaged in a task we feel uncertain about – where there is evidence to suggest that we might fail or lack competence. Human beings tend to be quick to judge, and we're especially quick to judge ourselves. If anything about our past performance in a certain area gives us cause for concern, we can form what's known as a limiting belief. These limiting beliefs come in all shapes and sizes, but their impact on our mindset can be huge. We can easily create a false paradigm based on inconsistent or incomplete evidence, and this false paradigm can be difficult for us to shift. A misinterpreted piece of feedback becomes 'My boss doesn't like me'. A mediocre performance in your last meeting becomes 'People never listen to me'. A bad experience as a child during the school play becomes 'I'm not good at public speaking'. In an attempt to spare ourselves from future pain, we generalise, delete and distort our actual experience and construct a reality that isn't only unhelpful but can also seriously damage our ability to succeed.

If we want to perform at our best, we have to seek out these limiting beliefs and challenge them. We have to recognise them for what they are: manifestations of our fears and not our reality. The starting point is simply to acknowledge that they exist. Ask yourself what's holding you back. Think about the situations where you know you're not achieving your full potential or the areas of your life that you would like to improve. What is it that's stopping you? How are you getting in your own way? Get as specific as possible. Sometimes it's really hard to meet these things head-on, but the results are worth the effort.

When I made the decision to retrain as a coach, I had several limiting beliefs about how my closest friends and family would judge me. I believed they would feel let down and think that I had given up on a promising career as an actor. I believed they wouldn't respect me as much if I followed my new passion. It took several sessions working with my own coach before I concluded that these beliefs were just false fears holding me back. I had to take each thing that scared me and confront it head-on. Of course my friends and family would support me; they'd been with me through all the highs and lows of my acting career, so why would they desert me now? How could a career that involved helping other people fulfil their potential be seen as something negative? One of the things they respected most was the fact that I'd always followed my passion; a new direction would reinforce that respect rather than diminish it. Once I was able to cut myself free from those invisible bonds, I never looked back.

Another key saying from my drama-school training was the phrase 'Get out of your own way and leave yourself alone'. One of my favourite acting teachers said this time and time again in the rehearsal room, but when I first heard it, I remember dismissing it as nonsense. What did it mean and how could I possibly put it into practice? It took me a couple of years to realise what a powerful idea it is. Most of us spend a lot of time getting in our own way. We put up invisible barriers for ourselves and make life harder than it needs to be. As an actor creating a character, you need to find freedom and flow, and the biggest enemy to your achieving this elusive state is your internal dialogue. When you judge yourself, when you hold on to limiting beliefs about your talents and your self-worth, you inhibit your ability to create. This is true in the context of acting and it's true in the context of every other profession I've ever encountered. Whether you're the CEO or the receptionist, in sales or in engineering, working for a multinational corporate or for a local charity, you need to free yourself from your negative and unhelpful self-talk.

When you're able to acknowledge and name your limiting beliefs, you're able to rationalise them. Think about the belief that's holding you back and ask yourself if the opposite has ever been true. For example, if your belief is that no one listens to your ideas, ask yourself if there has ever been a time when someone did. All you need is one piece of evidence to the contrary, one example that calls your assumptions into question, and you can blow your limiting belief out of the water. Pay especially close attention to the linguistic format of your thoughts. Words such as 'never', 'always' and 'everyone' suggest imperatives and absolutes which need to be challenged if they're getting in your way. Have you ever? Is it always? Was anyone the exception to the rule? How you talk to yourself matters just as much as how you talk to others, so pay attention to the language that you use.

Know your buttons

Hindsight is a wonderful thing. How many times have you looked back on a bad experience and realised that the outcome was inevitable, that a seemingly unstoppable series of events led to what happened? The problem is that when you're in the middle of the action, you're unaware of the pattern. You don't always spot what's coming down the line. We think our experience is a series of coincidences, but when we scratch beneath the surface, we see that we're fairly predictable. A great deal of how we react under pressure is pre-programmed. Just like Pavlov's dogs, we respond unconsciously to the stimuli we're exposed to. If you want more control over your behaviour, you have to understand what I call your 'buttons'.

Your buttons are your triggers. They can be pressed by situations or individuals, and when they are, your reactions are often instant and irrational. I like to visualise the big red flashing self-destruct button you find in movies like *Austin Powers*. There's always a label that reads 'Do Not Press', and yet we just can't seem to help ourselves. Without really thinking about it, we let events get the better of us and react explosively.

We must acknowledge that our buttons exist, just as we must acknowledge our limiting beliefs. Once we start to understand the sorts of things that cause us to react in unhelpful ways, we can start to do something about them. Think about situations where you often have a negative reaction or where your mindset doesn't support your objective. What is it that kickstarts these feelings? Is it the situation? Is it the environment? Is it the behaviour of others? Work this out so that you can spot the early warning signs. It might be the way a direct report asks questions in meetings or the tone of voice the CEO uses when she's unhappy with your results. Whatever your buttons are, make sure you define them as specifically as possible and then use your new-found knowledge to shield yourself from their effect.

By understanding our buttons and bringing them into our consciousness when we're under pressure, we start to create choice. We put space between the stimulus and our response. We stop working on autopilot and can decide how to react to the situation. A little bit of planning can go a long way when it comes to removing the element of surprise that these triggers can have; it will put you back in the driving seat, so you can make a more informed decision about how to respond.

ACT OF COMMUNICATION

• •

DISCOVER YOUR BUTTONS

When we have a consistently negative response to a situation or an individual, it's useful to understand our triggers. What are the circumstances or behaviours that cause us to unconsciously react this way? Once we know our 'buttons', we can put a plan in place to avoid them. Think about a situation where you would like to react differently – in a regular meeting, when closing a sale, while giving a speech – and then answer these questions:

1. What are your buttons? What is the trigger that sets you off?

2. What are the early warning signs? Is there a pattern you can identify?

3. What can you do to minimise your reaction? Can you pause and take a deep breath or choose another way to react?

Use this knowledge to put a plan in place for the next time you find yourself in the same situation. As soon as you spot the early warning signs, you can start to break the pattern.

• •

Use the two-minute rule

Another useful tool when you find yourself in an unhelpful headspace is the two-minute rule. None of us are perfect and there are bound to be times when no amount of planning or mindfulness can prevent us from going to the dark side. Try as we might, our emotions get the better of us and we start to lose control. As human as this reaction is, the danger is that we get stuck there, holding on to the negative feelings and finding ourselves unable to move forward. This can become a massive drain on our energy and time, and it can seriously undermine the impact that we make. The two-minute rule helps you acknowledge the reality that you find yourself in and then move through it.

Very simply, next time something goes wrong, or you're angry, or frustrated or disappointed, instead of trying to manage or defuse your emotions, lean in and even amplify them. It's really important to note that this must be done in a way that doesn't affect others. I'm not encouraging you to reach across the table and grab the person who's frustrating you or to behave in an offensive manner. Ideally, the two-minute rule technique should be carried out in private, or at least among people you trust. For two minutes, allow yourself to experience whatever negative emotions or thoughts you're having. If you want to vocalise or physicalise how you feel, go for it. Stomp your feet, scream, growl and get what you're feeling off your chest. As soon as the two minutes are over, stop. Move on. No going back. No going over old ground or bringing the topic up later. It's over. Move forward.

I found this technique invaluable when dealing with the regular rejection involved in auditioning for roles. As an actor, you have to fully invest yourself in each project you audition for. You have to live and breathe the character, and it's always an emotional roller coaster. You imagine yourself playing the part, cashing the pay cheque and winning the rave reviews. But the reality is that 90% of your life as an actor is spent auditioning for parts you don't get. You're having a great week if you manage to have three unsuccessful auditions because it means you're in the running rather than watching from the sidelines. Each time I got a no, the two-minute rule helped me deal with the disappointment and get straight back on the horse.

Control the frame

Once you've got some strategies for quieting the voices in your head, you're ready to get onto the field of play. Communication should always be a two-way process. Even in a presentation situation where only one party is speaking, it's still important to think of things as a dialogue. To make the dialogue effective, each party must understand their role and the rules of the game. The great thing from a communication perspective is that, if you're the one speaking, you have an opportunity to set those rules. I call this 'controlling the frame'.

Uncertainty is a trigger for anxiety in you and your audience. If you want to control your mindset, you need to be able to understand how to measure success and, ultimately, how to win. Setting the frame for a conversation allows you to be in the driving seat. It's not about dominating or beating others – it's about ensuring that everyone has clarity and certainty about what's taking place. Far too often I observe conflict situations where communication has broken down purely because no one really understands the rules. People fail to make an impact and lose their confidence because they haven't set out their expectations in advance. One of the simplest things you can do at the start of any conversation is articulate how you would like it to play out. Once you've given an interaction a 'frame', you can then seek confirmation that the other parties present will uphold the rules you've proposed.

Let me give you an example. For many people, being on the receiving end of a difficult question during a presentation is a nightmare situation that can throw them off track. If you pre-frame the presentation by saying, 'I'm going to take you through my slides, and I'll ask you to keep any questions until the end so that I can answer them all together', it will be much easier to push back when someone interrupts you in the middle of your flow. This technique works even better if you finish your framing with the magic phrase 'Is that OK?' If everyone says yes or nods in agreement, then you've gained their express permission to hold them to the rules. And if someone refuses to agree to your frame upfront, you can work to resolve the situation before you begin and get agreement as to how you'll proceed. In my experience, though, this has never been a problem; people will always agree to your pre-frame if you position it in the right way.

Here are some useful frames to consider:

Schedule frame

Use a schedule frame to clarify timings and the agenda. Make it explicit so that people know what to expect in advance and can tell where they are in the proceedings. If you detail this clearly at the outset, including how long each section/agenda item will last, you'll avoid people being distracted or worried that something important will be missed. It also allows timings to be negotiated at the beginning of a conversation, so the discussion doesn't get hijacked halfway through.

Open frame

If you want continual interaction and free-flowing conversation, encourage an open frame. Let people know that you expect questions and are happy for them to be posed at any time. This frame encourages creativity and collaboration.

Structure frame

A structure frame allows you to stipulate how you will interact with your audience. Communicate the roadmap for the conversation or presentation and make the boundaries around interaction and questions explicit. This frame encourages precision and order.

Outcome frame

When dealing with problems or situations that can be divisive, it's beneficial to focus the conversation using an outcome frame. This allows you to position the desired result and then focus the conversation on finding ways to achieve it. This frame helps to prevent the conversation from getting stuck on the problems being faced or the reasons why something can't be done.

Discovery frame

A discovery frame is a request for the suspension of judgement. This frame is especially useful when you want to encourage creativity and lateral thinking. It allows you to ask questions and generate new ideas without the pressure of being right. The aim is not to arrive at a solution but to gain the deepest possible understanding of the current situation and the options available.

'As if' frame

Think of this frame as an opportunity to take a no-obligation test drive. Actors act 'as if', so they can step into a character's shoes, and this technique is incredibly useful to help you understand the consequences of a specific action. When setting an 'as if' frame, ask the audience to imagine that a specific outcome has already been achieved. You can then begin to explore the resulting possibilities and implications.

Backtrack frame

Often, it's useful to have the option to rewind and look back. The backtrack frame allows you to check for understanding and confirm commitments. It's also useful for restarting a conversation after a disagreement, as you can use it to draw a line in the sand and proceed from the point directly before any conflict arose.

Whatever frame you choose, ensure that you make it explicit and get buy-in from everyone else involved. It's perfectly normal to switch frames several times during a conversation. Just make sure your audience knows which frame applies, so they know which rules to play by. When you do, you'll find that the voices in your head have much less to talk about and you can focus on the real conversation at hand.

Look for quick wins

Another great way to boost your confidence is to set yourself a 'quick win' early on in a conversation. Choose something simple that you can achieve within the first two minutes of your interaction. It could be not falling over as you walk onto stage, remembering the names of everyone you're meeting or perfectly reciting the opening line of your pitch. When you focus on these early victories, you ensure that you start proceedings on a positive note. You also trigger your body to give itself a healthy hit of dopamine, which makes you feel good. This is a great way to reduce nerves or anxiety in high-stakes environments and helps you quickly get into a state of flow. After my experience on set with Sir Michael Gambon, whenever I stepped in front of a camera or on stage, I would always set myself the target of speaking my first line without getting tongue-tied. Once I'd done that, I knew I could relax and start to enjoy the show.

Pack a parachute

My final piece of advice on mindset is to always be prepared. Communication is a live art, and things can (and frequently do) go wrong. The difference between good and great communicators is how well they deal with these mishaps. One of the best pieces of advice I ever received is 'Remember that your audience has no idea what you're going to say next'. Unless you're reading from a script that has been circulated in advance, no one has a clue what's about to come out of your mouth. This means you can't really get it wrong. If you don't tell or show people that you've made a mistake, they'll never know. Your job is to stop the voices in your head from taking control and derailing your performance.

So what do you do when the worst happens and you forget what's coming next or you find yourself in a cul-de-sac that you're having difficulty getting out of? You pull the cord on your parachute of course. Think of yourself as an elite fighter-jet pilot. If the worst happens and you need to press the eject button, you better hope that you packed a parachute. From a communication-skills perspective, your parachute is something you've planned in advance to get you out of a tricky spot. It might be a strategically placed glass of water that you can sip from to buy you enough time to find your next thought. It might be a pre-prepared question that you put to the audience. It might be a glance at your notes, a joke, a recap of what you've covered so far or even the suggestion of a coffee break so that you have time to regroup. Whatever it is, it's important that you pack it in advance, and if you want to be extra safe, it's always worth packing more than one. Spending a couple of minutes planning your parachute before a meeting, one-to-one or presentation could save you a lot of pain. The hope is that you never have to use it, but knowing that it's there is surprisingly reassuring and will be the difference between you looking cool, calm and collected or walking away with egg on your face.

ACT OF COMMUNICATION

● ●

CHOOSE YOUR PARACHUTE

Think about the next important communication scenario you're likely to find yourself in. It could be a meeting, a presentation or a one-to-one. What emergency planning do you need to do? Take some time to answer these questions:

1. What might go wrong? What do you hope won't happen?

2. How would you normally react if it did?

3. What could you do differently to get a better outcome?

4. What do you need to prepare in advance to achieve this better outcome? What is your parachute?

You might need to write out a list of the worst questions people could possibly ask and prepare your answers. You might need to ensure that you have a bottle of water and a glass handy in case of a dry mouth. You might need to speak to someone who will be in the audience and ask them to have a question ready to kick off the Q&A. Your parachutes will be unique to your circumstances. Do what it takes to ensure that you're ready for any eventuality.

• •

Get clear and focused

Your mindset can propel you forward or it can hold you back. If you want to create maximum impact, you need to learn how to control it and make it serve you. Take time to understand your patterns and what makes you tick. What are your habits? What is your default posture and what effect does it have? How do you breathe under pressure? How do your beliefs and buttons dictate your performance? Awareness unlocks the door to growth. Once you understand your behaviour, you can start to adjust and change it. When do you need to implement the two-minute rule? Are you in control of the frame? Can you identify some quick wins? And have you packed a parachute? With these things in place, you create space in your head. You make room for clarity and focus. You start to be able to direct your attention and take responsibility for your communication, ensuring that you take charge of the situation and find your flow.

Chapter Three

PRESENCE

Be seen and heard

There are some people who make an impact effortlessly. They walk into a room and you instantly know that they're there. You hear their voice and their message resonates. There are others who are almost invisible. You barely notice them and they hardly make a sound. The first group has presence. The second lacks it. The good news is that presence can be learned. It's something that you can develop and grow, and it's the third vital ingredient of impact.

Most people focus on their message – they agonise over their content, they worry about how to articulate their ideas for their audience. This is incredibly important, but it shouldn't be your primary focus. Before you worry about what to say, you must first think about how you say it, and the 'how' starts with the way you show up.

We've already established that you send out physical signals to your audience. The question is, are those signals telling those watching you that you're confident and in control? You don't have to be a massive extrovert and dominate the room. Some of the most impactful people I know would class themselves as quiet and reserved. However, they ensure they connect in an authentic way and let their audience see them.

Most people assume that because I was an actor, I'm an extrovert who loves walking into new social situations. In fact, that couldn't be further from the truth. In my personal life I'm quite introverted and prefer time for quiet reflection. But I've learned to get comfortable standing in the spotlight and can now choose to turn that side of myself up if I need to. If you want to make an impact, you must make a conscious choice about which side of yourself you reveal to your audience. Are you prepared to be seen and heard?

Presence has two parts: what you do physically and what you do vocally. They're closely linked but it's useful to look at them separately. When you have physical presence, people see your impact. When you have vocal presence, people hear your impact. If you want to perform at your best, you need both.

Stay in the moment

Presence isn't just about first impressions. It's about how you show up in every interaction you have. In simple terms, having presence is about being present. If you want to increase your presence, get used to being in the moment. As our diaries get fuller and fuller, it's easy to attempt to multitask, to allow our minds to wander from what we're doing now. How often do you find yourself thinking about a conversation that you've just had or are about to have instead of connecting 100% with the person in front of you?

The practice of mindfulness has grown in recent years as a direct response to this problem. It's all too common to focus on what's going on far outside of ourselves and fail to notice what's going on in our immediate vicinity. I'll never forget a simple question the principal of my drama school asked: 'How many trees did you pass on the way in this morning?' He posed it casually during a class on stagecraft. I had walked the same mile-long route over two hundred times and yet had no idea what was right in front of my nose. The next day I counted. The answer was twenty-seven. What are you failing to notice? Do you really see everything that's in front of you? When you make the effort to increase your awareness and be more in the moment, you instantly increase your presence.

Time is a finite resource. You therefore must be both strategic and generous in how you use it. I'm not going to go into the details of time management – I'm sure you don't need me telling you how to manage your diary – but I encourage you to be conscious of how you interact with others. If you don't have time for a 'quick chat' with someone, push back and ask them to schedule something in when you do. If you're in a meeting or dialling into a conference call, turn off all other devices and notifications and put all your focus on being in the moment. The concept of multitasking is a fallacy. If you want to be known as someone who makes an impact, focus on the here and now.

Take time out

Another key to presence is ensuring that you don't allow the lines between one interaction and the next to blur. Look at most people's diaries and you'll see their time is booked back to back. One meeting finishes and the next begins. They speed down corridors from meeting room to meeting room, take calls while driving to their next appointment, and send emails from their mobile device while dashing out to get some lunch. This becomes a real problem when the interactions begin to bleed into one another.

Imagine that you have an 8.30am meeting with a particularly tricky individual. Things get heated and you leave the room sixty minutes later angry and frustrated. The sensible thing would be to take a few minutes to regroup, calm down and get your thoughts back to the task at hand. The reality for most people is quite different. You would likely walk out of the meeting and immediately jump on the phone or head straight into your next appointment carrying all the baggage from your previous encounter.

In this situation, the more mentally and physically present you can be, the better. Taking thirty seconds to literally shake off the bad meeting will pay dividends. Seize the opportunity to break state, to reboot the system. Bring your consciousness to your physicality. Move, stretch and breathe. By resetting the body, you'll reset the mind. This practice will help you ring-fence each interaction you have, ensuring that you're fully present with each new audience. Get into the habit of pausing for a couple of seconds before you walk into a new room or dial a new number. Breathe slow and low, focusing on your intention. I guarantee you'll get better outcomes if you do.

Discover what 'good' looks like

Think about how you use your body on a daily basis. If you're anything like the average office worker, you probably spend at least five hours a day hunched in front of a screen, tapping at your keyboard. You probably spend another three hours sitting around a meeting room table or speaking on your phone. All these activities make us small. Our bodies close and contract. In the research community, this physicality is known as the 'iHunch'. We're literally devolving back to our caveman posture.

When we communicate with openness and transparency, we create engagement. The physical messages we send out should reflect this. It may feel comfortable to fold your arms or cross your legs, but you need to be aware of how these actions can be perceived. When relationships are strong, it might not matter at all, but if you're in a first-meeting or a high-pressure situation, you may come across as defensive or closed.

Great leaders are often said to have gravitas. What this actually means is that they allow gravity to work through the body. The easiest way to achieve this is to develop a 'neutral' posture while standing or sitting. This type of physicality allows you to take up just the right amount of space and ensures that you appear both powerful and relaxed.

Neutral stance:

1. Stand with your feet hip-width apart. This means that your hips, knees and feet are all aligned.

2. Balance the weight equally across the feet. Your weight should also be equally distributed between the toes and the heels.

3. Soften the knees. As soon as the knees are engaged, tension spreads into the thighs and buttocks. Imagine you're standing on a train – you need

to keep your knees relaxed so that you don't fall over. That's the level of relaxation to aim for. Keep checking back in, as many people tend to lock the knees when they're under pressure.

4. Make sure that the hips are centred. Be careful not to thrust the pelvis forward or push it backwards, or to lean to one side.

5. Imagine yourself lengthening through the spine and allow the shoulders to be heavy, arms hanging down by your sides.

6. Lengthen and free the neck. Imagine a piece of string pulling you up towards the ceiling from the crown of the head. You should feel as if you're standing tall but relaxed.

7. Smile. For some reason people get very serious when attempting this posture for the first time. Enjoy the feeling of being connected to the floor while stretching up towards the sky. When you take up space like this, you come across as having a huge amount of presence.

Neutral sitting:

1. The foundation for great seated posture is the same as for great standing posture: both feet on the floor, hip-width apart. In fact, if you go through the steps above and then lower your bottom into the chair, you've pretty much got it.

Many of us cross our legs when seated, or tuck our feet under our seat. This hugely diminishes our impact when the stakes are high and also makes it difficult for us to breathe from the diaphragm. So, keep your feet grounded and adjust the chair height or move forward on the seat if necessary, to allow you to achieve this.

2. Sit up on your sitting bones. And rather than sitting back into the chair, sit with a gap between you and the backrest so that you're forced to support yourself and take up your full height. This will stop you from slouching and make you appear more energised.

3. Lengthen and free the neck. Just like when you stand, imagine your head floating up towards the ceiling.

4. Create space between you and the table. Many people sit too close to the furniture. Make sure your wrists can rest on the table top but ensure that your torso isn't squeezed in. You'll appear more in command and will have space to move and address everyone in the room.

The techniques above come into their own in high-stakes situations, but to make your postures appear authentic, you need to practise them when the stakes are low. Try using neutral sitting at your desk first thing in the morning as you check your emails, or using neutral stance as you queue for your morning coffee. Whether sitting or standing, the most important thing is to have both feet on the ground and your weight equally distributed. Not only does this help your breathing, as we discovered when we looked at mindset, but it also sends out a signal to your audience that you're balanced and grounded. Quite simply, the more open and grounded you are, the more presence you will have.

To watch my video about neutral stance and neutral sitting, visit www.inflow.global/posture

Get assertive

Most people want to be liked. In many situations we fear coming across as aggressive or threatening. We therefore tend to shy away from behaviour that could be perceived in that way. And rightly so – influencing through fear is not something I would recommend. However, there is one flaw in this softly, softly approach. Most of us are bad judges of our own behaviour. We have poor calibration skills when it comes to assessing our impact.

There's a material difference between behaviour that's assertive and behaviour that's aggressive. While we don't want to stray into the aggressive territory, it's crucial to be able to display the assertive side of our character. Many people I work with confuse the two. They feel that if they develop a more assertive physicality, they'll be perceived as posing a threat. But if they're doing it properly, that's never the case.

When assessing the emotional state of other human beings, we unconsciously pick up on signals from three parts of the body – the feet, the shoulders and the head. If you ask a group to adopt a passive body position, most people will assume a narrow stance, allow the shoulders to collapse forward, and gaze towards the floor, bringing their head down as well. Ask them to adopt an aggressive body position and the stance will widen, the shoulders will be pulled back slightly, and the head will come up with the chin raised. Ask them to take a present posture and the stance will be grounded, the shoulders will be centred, and the head will be balanced too. When you're present, you inhabit your space without making yourself any bigger or smaller than you need to be. Positive assertiveness is just an extension of this. You must learn to hold your ground both physically and metaphorically. As long as you don't step into anyone else's territory, you won't be perceived as aggressive.

ACT OF COMMUNICATION

• •

TAKE A STANCE

If you want to increase your presence and gravitas, you need to pay attention to how you use your body. How do you normally stand? How do you normally sit? It's important to understand your habitual patterns first. Then, armed with your observations, you can start to make some changes.

Step 1: Notice

As you go about your daily business, pay attention to your posture. Do you cross your legs? Do you fold your arms? Do you push your weight into one hip? How do you sit at your desk? How do you walk down the corridor? Find somewhere quiet to sit and scan your body for tension. Where are the muscles sore or tight? Pay attention to these parts of the body and allow them to relax. As you continue with your day, do they get tight and tense again? If so, these are areas that will need your focus.

Step 2: Change

Once you've identified where you habitually hold tension in the body, it's time to actively work to reduce it. Find time each day to give those areas a stretch or give yourself a quick massage. As most of us spend large portions of our days in front of screens and typing at keyboards, we tend to carry lots of tension in the neck and shoulders – pay particular attention to these areas. Also, spend at least five minutes each day standing or sitting in neutral stance. It's a tiny change but it will make a big difference to your impact.

• •

Stop thinking about your hands

When I'm running workshops and seminars, the question that I get asked most is 'What do I do with my hands?' My short answer is 'Nothing'. If you're sitting round the dinner table with family or chatting with friends in a bar, do you ever find yourself thinking, 'What should I do with my hands right now?' Of course not. Your gestures are instinctively connected to your content and your hands take care of themselves. But in high-stakes work situations, many people suddenly become self-conscious. Their hands end up in their pockets, on their hips, behind their backs or in myriad other strange locations. This can limit expression and make it look as if you have something to hide.

So, what should you do instead? My advice is to avoid repetitive gestures and fixed positions at all costs. Get used to having your hands loosely hanging by your sides. When the impulse takes you, commit to whatever gesture feels appropriate and then allow the arms to go back to their natural resting place at the side of the body. When working with clients, I often get initial pushback on this. I get told it feels strange and that other people will think it looks odd. When this happens, I ask people to think about every toddler they've ever encountered. Have you ever seen a two-year-old standing with their legs crossed and one hand on their hip? I very much doubt it. Young children are grounded in the way they walk. Their spines are long, their movement is fluid and their arms hang by their sides. This is the most ergonomic and free way of using our bodies. The skeleton in the biology lab doesn't have its arms crossed.

Keeping your hands in front of or behind the body closes you off from your audience and can send out unconscious signals of defensiveness. It's much better to stay relaxed and open. You may feel a little vulnerable, but with vulnerability comes power. You send a message to your audience that they needn't be afraid of you but that you're not scared of them either. I see it as the ultimate display of power and authority, and it's so easy to do.

Expand your bubble, expand your influence

A useful way to think about your physical presence is to imagine that you're walking around in your very own protective bubble – that you're surrounded by a perfect sphere and that you own all the space 360 degrees around you. Imagine yourself inside a Zorb or think of Leonardo da Vinci's *Vitruvian Man* and you've got the right idea.

Under pressure, many people allow their bubble to collapse or deflate; they become smaller and their impact and influence diminishes. I once used this visualisation technique with a CEO who hated public speaking and would break out into a sweat whenever she walked on stage. Before we worked together, she associated physical expansiveness with being aggressive and therefore often made herself small in an attempt to be liked. By visualising her bubble, she was able to walk out in front of her audience without any of her usual fear. She asserted her right to be on stage and her audience saw her as powerful and in control.

Your bubble doesn't need to repel other people or put a barrier between you and them. In fact, it's quite possible to maintain your bubble while shaking hands or sitting in a meeting room. The important thing is to keep expanding your bubble into the space and not allow anyone to burst it! When you own the space around you, you increase your ability to influence.

ACT OF COMMUNICATION
• •

TAKE UP SPACE

Before your next meeting, spend thirty seconds visualising your bubble. Make sure that you make it as expansive as possible. Enjoy the sensation of taking up more room. Let your body fill the space. Your challenge is to maintain this expansion during the meeting, regardless of the outcome of the conversations. Notice how your new physicality impacts your mental state.

• •

Look into their eyes

Think about the last person you spoke to face-to-face. Could you tell me their eye colour? If you couldn't, then I'd question if you really connected with them. They say that the eyes are the window to the soul. If you want to engage with people on more than just a superficial level, you need to make sure that you really see them.

I vividly remember the day I met Bill Clinton. I use the word 'met' lightly – I'm certain that he wouldn't remember me, but I'll never forget the encounter. I was twenty years old and happened to be walking through Oxford one afternoon when I noticed a bit of commotion further down the street. Curiosity got the better of me, and I jostled through the crowd to see what was going on. To my surprise, there was the former president of the United States walking down the middle of the road towards me. His daughter was at University College and he was in town to visit her. His presence was palpable. What he did was so simple and so powerful. As he walked through the crowd, he made meaningful eye contact and smiled. He didn't speak to anyone or shake any hands. He simply connected, and as a result, every single person in his presence felt special. It was a masterclass in impact and the importance of eye contact.

What we can all learn about effective communication from Bill Clinton is the value of connecting with others through the eyes. It's a two-way transaction – the transfer of energy between two people. Think of eye contact as a gift. You're giving something special to the person you're looking at. If you'd bought a present for a loved one, you wouldn't throw it at them – you'd hand it to them gently and make sure they'd received it before you took your hands away.

When I'm coaching, I ask my clients to think about eye contact lasting for the length of a thought. Once they've delivered the whole thought to a single person, they can move on and find the next person to interact with. This works especially well when you have large audiences, as the four or five people sitting around the person you're focusing on will feel as if you're speaking directly to them too. Don't worry about how many seconds you've been looking at someone; instead make sure that you're investing your thoughts in them. Not only does this show the audience that you're present, it also ensures you keep your head up, which improves your posture and keeps your body language open.

Act 'as if'

In the Mindset chapter, I talked about the 'as if' frame. Acting 'as if' is also an excellent tool for transforming your physical presence. Your imagination is a powerful resource. If you accept that the mind and body are linked, you can start to use the mind to change the body. As an actor, you use your imagination to create a character. You find a role model or an image of what the character you're playing might look like. Then you start to use your body to act them out. Just like children playing a game of make-believe, actors change their physicality to embody a part.

In life we play many different roles – our work role is just one of them. As well as being a communication-skills trainer, I'm also a father, a husband, a CEO, a professional speaker and an allotment gardener. All these roles have a slightly different physicality. I sit and stand differently around the boardroom table than I do on stage or when I'm at home with my wife and daughter. It's still me. I'm not acting. I'm just bringing different parts of myself to the situation.

Like an actor, you too can act 'as if' in different situations. Imagine who would deal well with the scenario you find yourself in and bring a bit of that person to the table. You might imagine someone you know and admire or think about a famous politician or a celebrity. Who displays the type of behaviour you'd like to have? Would Sheryl Sandberg deal well with this set of circumstances? What would Richard Branson say at this moment? How would Angela Merkel react right now? Imagine them in your shoes and act 'as if'. Notice how it changes what you do with your body language and your performance. It's not guaranteed to work perfectly, but it will guarantee a different outcome. After all, if you always do what you always did, you'll always get what you always got.

Be at Level 8

Energy is the currency of communication. So, how much or how little do you bring into the room? Think of communication as the transfer of energy between two parties. If you have an idea that you want to communicate, you need to bring it to life in the hearts and minds of the people you're communicating with. If you don't, the idea dies. If you want to be a great communicator, you must energise your thoughts and take responsibility for energising your audience too. No one else will do it for you.

I know the concept of energy can sound a bit 'out there', but it's something we all understand instinctively and are probably mostly unaware of. I want you to imagine energy as having a scale. Think of the volume dial on an old-fashioned radio: 1 is the lowest and 10 is the highest. At Level 1, it's like you have 'man flu'; you can't get out of bed and you can hardly move or make a sound. At Level 10, it's like you've had two energy drinks and a bar of chocolate; you're slightly wired and bouncing off the walls. Most of us operate somewhere in the middle: a Level 5. The problem with Level 5 is that it's not very dynamic. It's a safe way to cross the road but unlikely to make much of an impact. If we want to make an impression on our audience, we need to turn things up, and I recommend turning things up to a Level 8. Some of you might be thinking, 'Hold on a minute. That seems a little high. Why can't we stick with a Level 6 or 7?' The rationale behind going to Level 8 is that, in my experience, most people have poor calibration skills. They overestimate their energy levels and underestimate how much energy it takes to engage their audience. Level 8 means you're on. It means you're leading the room and you're fully committed to what you're talking about. Great communication costs you energy.

A word of warning about Level 8 energy, though. You have to be sensitive with how you use it. Level 8 is your end goal, but it's not always your starting point. How many meetings have you been to where everyone around the table is at a Level 3? If you walk into that room and start at a Level 8, there's a good chance that your audience will switch off or leave. You run the risk of your energy putting others on the back foot. So, if you want to increase your influence, get used to pacing and leading. Be aware of your audience's energy level, go in one level above, and then start to warm them up.

Finding your voice

Now that you've explored your physical presence, I want to ask you a strange but important question. What does your impact sound like? If you're anything like 99% of the population, listening to the sound of your voice is an uncomfortable experience for you. Even as a trained actor, I find hearing a recording of myself speaking or watching myself back on video excruciating! Yet the camera and the voice recorder don't lie. You need to get over the self-consciousness involved in experiencing your own sound and begin to consider what your voice says about you as a communicator.

What we sound like, our vocal presence, plays a huge part in building our credibility and generating trust. You don't have to like how you sound, but your audience does. Certain voices instantly make us feel at ease, and others put us on edge. We could listen to certain people talk forever, and we can't wait for others to stop. Often, it's not what is said but how it is said that counts. One actor can speak the lines in Hamlet to rave reviews while another can utter the same words and find their performance condemned.

Finding your voice is crucial to making your message land. It's how you bring your ideas to life in the hearts and minds of others. The good news is that the voice can be trained. It's a muscle that can be exercised and strengthened. Former British prime minister Margaret Thatcher famously had voice coaching to lower her tone and give her voice more gravitas. Love her or loathe her, her vocal transformation was remarkable and led to the perception of her as a more powerful leader. Developing your vocal presence will help you authentically play your role. You don't need to sound like an actor or have a deep, booming tone – you just need to speak in a way that helps you connect to the words you're saying and makes others want to listen.

Speak on a full tank

As we discussed in the Mindset chapter, as well as being a brilliant tool for calming our nerves, the breath is also the fuel for the voice. In casual conversation it's unusual for us to run out of breath. We think a thought, breathe for that thought and then speak it aloud without needing to snatch for air. The breath and the thought are inextricably linked. The *Oxford English Dictionary* defines 'inspiration' as both 'a sudden brilliant or timely idea' and 'the drawing in of breath'. The root is the Latin word *inspirare*, which means 'to breathe'. If we want to make sure our ideas are heard, we need to make sure that we have plenty of fuel in the tank. We have to ensure that we're breathing from the diaphragm and using our full lung capacity to support the words we're speaking.

When working to increase your vocal presence, your starting point should be breath work. Make sure that the abdominals are relaxed, the throat is free and the air is able to simply drop in and out of the body. Yawning is a great way to check that everything is working correctly. Not a polite yawn, with the mouth hardly opened and a hand to cover your embarrassment, but a big theatrical yawn, mouth opened wide, teeth and tongue visible for all the world to see. You might want to perform the yawn in private, but it's important that you don't hold back. Once you've taken a couple of big, yawning breaths, focus your attention on your abdomen and make sure that each breath is filling the body with air.

Make your ideas resonate

Once the breath is in place, we can start focusing on using the voice to bring our words to life. To really make an impact on our audience, what we say has to resonate. This means that the words we speak need to vibrate with our audience. People must have a kinaesthetic experience of what we're saying. That might sound a little New Age, but our speech is made up of sound waves, and these sound waves are what the listener's brain converts into meaning. To hear our message, people need to feel our words.

In the world of voice coaching, we talk about the chest voice and the head voice. The people you identify as having strong vocal presence will normally have lots of chest resonance. The bass notes give the voice gravitas and authority. I'm not suggesting that you make your voice as low as possible but that you pay attention to where in the vocal register your voice normally sits. If you tend to produce a higher sound, which is common with females, you need to work on opening up the voice and increasing your resonance. It's important to be aware of any tension in the throat and jaw. If these areas are tight, your ability to create resonance is inhibited. The simplest way to counter this is to yawn in the theatrical way I described above.

We communicate emotions on our vowels. Vowels are the sounds of elation, excitement and pain. Think of a football supporter watching a game. When their team scores a goal, you'll hear a loud, resonant 'Yyeeeeeeeess!' not a short, clipped 'Yes'. If we want our voices to be more expressive, we need to get used to investing in our vowels and sharing them in a resonant way.

Increase your range

Boring delivery can kill the best ideas. Whether you're in a meeting, on the phone, giving a presentation or engaged in a one-to-one, you need to bring colour to the words you speak to create interest in your audience. One way of doing this is to explore the different pitches available to you. The average person has access to a vocal range of two octaves. That's fifteen notes at our disposal. Most of us use between three and five. That's not quite monotone, but it's not far off. You don't need to become an opera singer to be a great communicator, but you do need to think about the impact your range has on your message. Try visualising your voice as a graph of sound waves. If you're using only three to five notes, the waves will be fairly uniform and consistent. Now imagine the graph if you were using eight to ten notes. How much more interesting would it be? The more variation in sound waves you create, the more interesting your words become to the listener.

Challenge yourself to be more expressive with your voice. Can you use some of your higher notes as well as some of your lower ones? It may feel strange at first, but the more expressive your voice becomes, the more compelling your message will be. A simple trick to help the voice sound brighter is to smile slightly as you talk. I don't mean a full-blown grin – just keeping the jaw released and allowing the edges of the mouth to rise is enough to change the sound. When we smile, we naturally lift the soft palate at the roof of the mouth. This creates more space in the mouth for resonance and stops us from producing a nasal, flat sound. It also has the added bonus of making us appear happy and warm which, in 99% of situations, is a win-win.

ACT OF COMMUNICATION
• •

HUM A LITTLE TUNE

If you want to have more vocal impact, you need to work on increasing your resonance. Your voice is a muscle, so regular workouts will help strengthen it. While I was at drama school, I did fifteen to thirty minutes of vocal warm-up exercises nearly every day. In business you don't need to be so rigorous, but if you can find three to five minutes each day to focus on your voice, you'll hear the results quickly. A vocal warm-up is especially important if you have a critical meeting or phone call first thing in the morning. Our voices naturally warm up as we speak throughout the day, but first thing in the morning they can be particularly lacking in resonance and range.

The following exercise is a great start:

Spend three minutes gently humming along to your favourite song. Volume isn't the focus of this exercise; I just want you to concentrate on creating vibrations in the chest and throat. If it's helpful, place a hand on the larynx or the breastbone so that you feel what's happening in the body as you do the exercise. It's important to hum and not sing. Humming doesn't place any strain on the vocal folds. It's therefore a much gentler way to warm up your voice and will avoid tiring it before you use it for speaking. Try to choose a song that has a variety of pitches – some high notes and some low notes – so that you explore your full range. This is a great way to make sure your voice is functioning at full capacity for an important meeting, phone call or presentation.

To watch my video about increasing your vocal resonance and range, visit www.inflow.global/resonance

Articulate your message

Whatever your role in an organisation, it's important to give your audience two things: clarity and certainty. Whether you're trying to influence your peers, your direct reports or your managers, one of the worst things you can do is confuse. The ideas that you need to express might be complex, but if others can't follow your train of thought, the consequences can be significant. You need to be able to paint a picture of what you're trying to communicate in enough detail that the people who are listening can act upon your words. You therefore must become proficient at articulating your thoughts in a clear and compelling way.

Most of us don't think of ourselves as experts, and yet, we often know more about our area of a business than anyone else. Because we spend so much time and focus on our little bit of the jigsaw, we can take this knowledge for granted. This is especially true when communicating with people who are more senior. We assume that they're as knowledgeable as we are, and we tend to speed through our content as a result. This speed can be compounded by nerves. If we feel uncertain, or under pressure to perform, we get a hit of adrenaline and go even faster. This leaves our audience scrabbling to keep up and potentially confused. In this situation, one way to apply the metaphorical brake is to focus on your articulation.

There are forty-three muscles in the face. These muscles control your ability to get your mouth around words. If you want more control over the clarity of your message, you need to train these muscles to be more dexterous. Most actors incorporate some sort of face and tongue stretches into their daily warm-up, and I recommend that everyone I work with does the same. If you were with me in the car while I was on my way to an important meeting, you'd see me blowing through my lips, sticking out my tongue and contorting my face to get the blood pumping and ensure that I didn't trip over my words.

Regular articulation exercises help you be more deliberate with your message. When you're working hard to articulate your thoughts, it's much harder to rush. You turn the communication of your ideas into a physical act rather than just a mental one. This helps give your ideas weight and significance. Just as emotion is carried on vowel sounds, meaning is carried on the consonants. Your audience needs to hear each word fully and clearly to understand your message. Think about the best communicators you know – I bet they appear committed to the words they're speaking. When you articulate your thoughts clearly, you give them form. It's like putting them in a box and placing them in your audience's hands instead of throwing them in their general direction and hoping that they catch them.

ACT OF COMMUNICATION

• •

GET YOUR MOUTH AROUND THE WORDS

There are several exercises you can do to help improve your articulation. The important thing is to engage as many of the muscles of the face as possible to get the blood pumping. Try these exercises:

1. Open your mouth and make a surprised face, stretching everything as wide as you possibly can. Hold the pose for five seconds. Then screw up your face as tightly as possible, pushing everything towards your nose. Hold this pose for five seconds too. Repeat both poses three times.

2. Blow through your lips like a horse three times. Then smack your lips together ten times. Repeat both exercises three times.

3. The tongue is a huge muscle that should be mobilised to help you create clarity when you speak. Try sticking it out and writing your name in the air with it. Repeat three times.

I would highly recommend doing all of these exercises daily. You might wish to do them in private, but I've been known to do them all walking down the street, and I'm certain that no one has noticed.

Finally, think about incorporating a couple of tongue-twisters into your warm-up. Any childhood rhyme will do. 'Red lorry, yellow lorry' and 'Peter Piper picked a peck of pickled peppers' are two of my favourites.

• •

To watch my video about
improving your articulation, visit
www.inflow.global/articulation

Create a connection

It doesn't matter how perfect your message or your voice are if your audience doesn't hear them. Clients often ask me if they need to be louder. My standard reply is that they need to be more energised. You can whisper to a room full of 1,000 people and as long as you have enough energy in your voice, they'll all hear you. Yet, you can speak loudly in a room full of twenty and no one will listen. It's about how you direct your communication. How committed are you to making yourself heard?

The vocal energy you should bring to each interaction depends largely on the size of the audience. If you're speaking to a large group, you'll have to work harder to connect than if you were speaking to one or two people sitting close by. If you have a tendency to speak quietly, it's useful to imagine that the audience is 10–20% bigger than it actually is. The key is focusing on allowing your voice to reach everyone who's listening. When talking to large groups, we often focus only on the people in the first couple of rows. You need to ensure that you connect with everyone.

Committing to your message is a vulnerable act. When you send your ideas out into the world, there's a risk that others won't approve of them or will dismiss them. But great communicators stand by their words. They share them with conviction, and that conviction is reflected in the connection they make to the language. If you say 'I'm really excited to be here', your audience needs to feel your excitement. If they don't, they'll doubt your sincerity. The way to build trust is to deeply connect with what you're saying. You lead by example. If you can connect, others will too.

The power of the pause

The most underused tool in most communication toolkits is silence. Rarely do we make time to pause. Most people are scared to stop talking. In presentations, we worry that it will look as if we've lost our train of thought, and in meeting scenarios, we fear that the floor will be hijacked and someone else will take control of the conversation. As long as the pause is intentional and well used, the reality couldn't be further from the truth.

One of the major benefits of embracing silence in your communication is that it allows your audience time to think. If you speak too quickly or fail to put space around your ideas, your audience has to work too hard to keep up. When we hear things for the first time, we need a moment to process our thoughts. The most common question in the minds of those listening to you is 'What's in it for me?' As they try to make sense of new information, one of their first unconscious instincts is to assess how it affects them personally. Until they have performed this 'safety check', they aren't really listening to anything else.

If, for example, you introduce a big new concept in a meeting and then want to talk in detail about how it will be implemented, it's essential that you give people time to process in between. I'm not talking minutes. Just a couple of seconds of silence so they can get their thoughts in order before you move on to your next points. Using pauses in this way not only signposts the important parts of your message, it also shows that you're in command. All the best speakers use the pause effectively, and it's well worth investing some time and energy getting comfortable with deploying it.

ACT OF COMMUNICATION

• •

HEAD, SHOULDERS, KNEES AND TOES

When you want to make sure you're warmed up and ready to create maximum impact, use the nursery rhyme 'Head, Shoulders, Knees and Toes' as a reminder.

Head: Is your voice warmed up? Are the muscles of the face alive and engaged? Is the neck free and the head floating up towards the ceiling?

Shoulders: Are shoulders relaxed and open? Is the breath low in the body rather than held in the chest?

Knees: Are the knees soft and is the body free from tension?

Toes: Are the feet and toes hip-width apart and grounded? Is the weight balanced?

This is a great checklist to work through before engaging in any important communication.

• •

Step into the spotlight

When you focus on your physical and vocal presence, you ensure that you're ready to step into the spotlight when you need to perform. These are skills that can be developed. Behaviours that can be trained. Repetition helps you build habits and create muscle memories so that your body and voice know what to do under pressure. Presence is a vital ingredient of your impact, and it often requires you to step outside of your comfort zone, to be bigger and louder than you might otherwise feel comfortable with.

I'll always remember standing in the wings of the Minerva Theatre in Chichester waiting to make my professional stage debut. After three years of drama-school training and four weeks of rehearsal, I was about to step in front of a paying audience for the first time. Would they like what I did? Would I remember my lines? I could feel the nerves rising as we got closer and closer to curtain-up. The butterflies in my stomach. The dryness of my tongue in my mouth. But when the moment arrived and I stepped out and took centre stage, all the anxiety melted away. I'd done the work and now I could enjoy the performance.

Trust that your body knows what to do. Allow yourself to expand and take up space. Make sure that you're grounded, whether seated or standing. Let your hands take care of themselves. Expand your bubble. Connect with others through your eyes. If it helps, act 'as if'. Breathe. Give your words resonance and articulate them clearly. Explore your range and the power of the pause. Bringing your attention to these simple practices will change the way that you feel about yourself and the way that others perceive you.

Chapter Four

AUDIENCE

Walk in their shoes

The fourth ingredient of the IMPACT model is audience. When I use the word 'audience', I'm talking about anyone and everyone you come into contact with. It could be an audience of one during an appraisal, an audience of twelve while meeting with the board, or an audience of two thousand when speaking at an industry conference. An audience can be internal or external. It can be made up of people you know well or people you're meeting for the first time. This diversity can often prove a challenge – it can be difficult to know how best to engage a particular audience. The key is to continually try to walk in their shoes. You have to adapt your approach to suit the individuals you're interacting with.

The quality of your performance is irrelevant if you're performing for the wrong audience. No matter how clear your intention, how focused your mindset, how strong your presence, if you don't understand whom you're speaking to, you'll find it difficult to succeed. I became very aware of this while working on the feature film *Thunderbirds*. I was playing Virgil Tracy, pilot of *Thunderbird 2*, a character many people in the UK grew up watching on their TV screens. About two weeks before we were due to start filming, I got a phone call from the late, great Bill Paxton, who was going to be playing my dad. He invited me and the other four young actors who were playing the Tracy brothers to hang out with him for the day in London. We spent several hours together exploring the city and discussing the project that we were going to be working on for the next four months. Bill was a true professional and, as part of his research, had immersed himself in the original puppet series. Having starred in some of the biggest movies of the preceding two decades, including *Aliens*, *Apollo 13*, *Twister* and *Titanic*, he had some important words of advice: 'Honour the audience'. He made it clear that if we wanted the film to be a success, we had to understand whom we were making it for. We had to get to know what the fans wanted and then we had to make sure that we delivered it for them.

When you're in the spotlight, it's too easy to think you're the most important person in the room. The reality, of course, is that your audience is much more important than you are. If you're a film actor, audiences pay your wages. They buy the cinema tickets. They decide with their feet and their reviews whether or not you become a box-office hit. In a business context, the same is true. If you don't win over your audience, you don't succeed. You always need them to buy or buy into your idea, whether you're on the phone, in a meeting, giving a presentation or delivering feedback. In every context you find yourself in, you need to make sure that you understand your audience inside out. Get to know what makes them tick. What they fear. What frustrates them. What they like and dislike. How they prefer to be communicated with. When you deeply understand who they are, you can truly start to make an impact.

Influence is not a dirty word

No matter what your job title is, you're always influencing others. You want people to listen to what you have to say. You want them to act upon your words. Sometimes the concept of influencing gets a bad reputation. People associate it with manipulating or duping people into doing things against their will. This is categorically not the sort of influencing I encourage my clients to practise. When connected to a clear intention, your ability to influence is a positive and necessary part of your communication toolkit. You must be able to take your audience on the journey with you.

If we accept the idea that we have influence regardless of what we do, surely it's better to be conscious about our choices. We need to be more in control of the signals that we send out to the world, of the language that we use and the energy we bring to the table. Whenever we speak, we're trying to change the hearts and minds of those we're communicating with. If we want to be effective at our jobs, we have to get used to making people think and feel different. That's the nature of effective communication. To create that change, we need to understand, or at least be able to predict, our audience's current thoughts and feelings.

Do your research

How well do you know your audience? Do you take time to consider their perspective? I'm always amazed at how little effort most people in business make to consider the people they're talking to. They fail to tailor their approach to the needs of their audience and focus instead on their own objectives and interests. In the world of theatre, the opposite is true. A creative team will spend lots of time understanding the target demographic, and the performance will be crafted to ensure that it resonates with that particular audience. A production of *Hamlet* at Shakespeare's Globe theatre will look and feel very different from the same play performed at an edgy venue like Trafalgar Studios. While the story and the words that the actors speak will be the same, the way these things are brought to life will differ enormously to appeal to the different types of audiences that each theatre attracts.

It's important, therefore, to do your research. What can you find out about the person or people you're speaking to? What do you know already? What new information would it be useful to have? I recommend that you play private detective and do as much digging as you can. You can even attempt to look at the people you spend a lot of time with in a new light. What do you know about them that would help you predict their future behaviour? A quick Google search can often bring up numerous results, and a trawl of social media profiles can give you great insight into their current thinking. I also recommend speaking to other people who have dealt with them before. Can you get the inside track? This isn't just a task for salespeople. Whether you're speaking to your boss, a room full of strangers at a conference, or a small delegation from a new supplier, finding out as much as possible about those you're speaking to pays dividends. It's especially useful to look for specific words and phrases that they use frequently so that you can play them back to them. The more you can 'speak their language', the more likely you are to create rapport.

I suggest that you break your research down into two parts: the facts and the feelings.

The facts comprise the empirical evidence about your audience – How old are they? What is their job title? How many years have they been with the company? What has their previous performance been like? This information helps you to build up a picture of their experience and interests.

The feelings are anecdotal observations and predictions – What is their reaction likely to be? What emotions might they display? How do others describe them? This level of detail gives you a deeper understanding of their behavioural patterns and helps you make informed decisions about how to adapt your performance for maximum influence.

ACT OF COMMUNICATION

• •

UNCOVER FACTS AND FEELINGS

Before your next meeting or important phone call, spend some time researching the person or people you're going to be talking with. Can you build up an accurate picture of who they are? Their likes and dislikes? Create two lists:

1. FACTS – What do I know?

2. FEELINGS – What do I sense?

How does this research alter your approach? Which pieces of information would be helpful to use in your interactions?

We trust people who are like us, so if you have any common ground with your audience, make sure you articulate it so that they know they're speaking with someone who is like-minded. Even something seemingly insignificant, such as a shared interest in a particular sport, can go a long way to building rapport and deepening your influence.

• •

Put people in boxes

I know that people hate being put into boxes, but in terms of planning how to engage and influence, it's an incredibly useful approach. When I trained to be an actor, we spent a lot of time working on archetypes to help us create characters, and I've taken that work and reverse-engineered it to help people understand their audience better.

I was lucky to be taught by Yat Malmgren, one of the great movement and acting teachers of the last fifty years. Yat taught legendary actors, such as Sean Connery, Anthony Hopkins, Colin Firth and Helen McCrory, and is the creator of a discipline called movement psychology. Yat's work brought together Jungian psychology with the movement technique of Rudolf Laban. I'd need to write another book to explain the details, but as an actor, it helped me understand the connection between what a character was thinking and how they behaved. Yat was able to codify the different energies that people had and how these energies influenced their performance. What I found fascinating was that while I could identify these archetypes in the scripts I was working on, I could also spot the characters in real life too.

Years later, when I started helping people to communicate more effectively, it dawned on me that if you could identify the different types of energies your audience showed up with, you could adapt your own performance and communication to appeal to that particular audience type. You could find a hidden language that would allow you to communicate at a deeper level. I looked for the common threads and identified four energy centres that people communicate from:

- The head
- The heart
- The gut
- The feet

Collectively, I called them the In Flow Energy Centres. If you want to deeply understand your audience, you have to understand where their energy is coming from.

Before we go any further, I want to acknowledge that we're all complex and unique individuals, and in order to survive, we use all four energy centres on a regular basis. However, each of us has a default position, a place of comfort that we go back to when we feel under pressure. Understanding your audience's default allows you to tap into their energy and breaks down potential resistance.

The In Flow Energy Centres

While we're all unique, each of us has a lot in common with our fellow human beings. Once we understand the four energy centres – the head, the heart, the gut and the feet – we can start to build on our commonalities to increase our influence. These four centres have very different qualities, and these qualities affect our behaviour. Once you know how to categorise these behaviours, you can quickly identify which energy centre they relate to. This makes it relatively easy to discern which centre your audience is working from. Then you can adapt your behaviour and even your language to better engage with your audience. It's important to note that all the energy centres are equally weighted and important. There is no 'preferred' centre. What's vital is that you recognise your default and then adapt your performance to suit your audience's energy.

Head

Head people are logical. They rely on their cognitive thought processes and critical analysis to interpret a situation rather than their emotional response or gut feeling. They're normally process driven and like an ordered approach. If a plan has been agreed, they'll work towards the outcome without deviating from it. They prefer to have all the information to hand when making a decision and normally take time to reflect on the data before doing so. They value precision and consistency and will approach tasks in a structured way.

In typical organisations, you'll find head people in the more procedural job areas, such as finance, quality assurance, IT and engineering.

When interacting with head people, you need to be able to justify the logic of your argument and produce evidence. It's best to provide documentation in advance so that they have time to digest it, otherwise they may not be forthcoming with an opinion. It's often useful to employ visual aids as well. When asking questions, give them time to process and formulate an answer – don't jump in to fill the silence.

Heart

Heart people are emotionally intelligent. They have a strong ability to connect to their feelings and will always consider the wider impact of any action. They are team focused and like to bring everyone along for the journey. Given a choice, they'll work in a collaborative way, and they value the opinions of others. In touch with their emotions, they're also adept at assessing the 'emotional temperature' of the room. They tend to communicate with compassion, focusing on building trust and meaningful relationships.

Those with a heart energy centre are often found in people-facing roles such as HR and customer services, where empathy and listening skills are important.

When interacting with heart people, it's useful to highlight the human side of your argument. What will the impact be on the team or the wider organisation? It's also effective to use inclusive language – 'we' and 'us' rather than 'you' and 'I'. Heart people like everyone to be heard and will prefer to work in a consultative way when trying to reach a decision.

Gut

Gut people are intuitive and tend to rely on instinct – their gut feeling – when making decisions. They like flexibility and value creativity. Options are important to gut people, and they'll push back against anything they regard as overly structured. They're good at understanding and articulating the big picture but less good at focusing on the details. Gut people thrive when they have multiple balls in the air, but they can struggle to complete projects as they get bored easily. Gut people often have lots of energy and are natural extroverts who relish the spotlight.

You'll find lots of gut people working in marketing and communications roles. You'll also find them in jobs where idea generation and an ability to deal with change are important.

When interacting with gut people, it's best to give them options and ask for their input. They respond well to storytelling and will quickly switch off if there's too much detail. They're happy to engage with loose frameworks that allow for some creativity but will feel constrained by rigid processes and procedures. Gut people perform at their best when they're working in an energetic, dynamic environment where their contributions are valued.

Feet

Feet people are driven and like to create forward momentum. They are highly motivated by clear goals, and once they understand their targets, they'll work tirelessly to achieve them. This drive tends to lead them to work at a fast pace, and they can get frustrated when they perceive others to be putting up roadblocks. Feet people have a strong ability to focus on the task at hand and aren't easily distracted. Often strong-willed and competitive, they can get impatient if things aren't progressing quickly enough. They find too much detail distracting and like to receive information in easily digestible chunks.

Feet people often work in sales roles or find themselves leading projects where their ability to identify and hit key milestones is invaluable.

When interacting with feet people, keep in mind that they respond well to definite language – 'we must', 'we will' – and look for brevity and specificity in an argument. They will much prefer hearing an overview and a few key action points to being taken through the complete reasoning behind a decision. The more direct you are, the better. If you can talk in terms of goals, deadlines and milestones, you'll appeal to their sense of drive.

The table below provides a useful overview of the In Flow Energy Centres. Use it to help you determine which default centre your audience uses.

THE IN FLOW ENERGY CENTRES

HEAD

Characteristics: Analytical. Detail focused. Logical. Precise. Consistent. Structured.

Attitude: Let's do it right.

Language:
- The evidence indicates that...
- What is the process for getting this done?
- How do we know that?

FEET

Characteristics: Driven. Outcome focused. Competitive. Purposeful. Strong-willed. Fast paced.

Attitude: Let's do it now.

Language:
- We have to make a decision.
- Will it move us towards our goal?
- I need this done ASAP.

HEART

Characteristics: Caring. Relationship focused. Supportive. Trusting. Reliable. Patient.

Attitude: Let's do it together.

Language:
- How does it feel to you?
- How will this affect the team?
- I feel...

GUT

Characteristics: Impulsive. Options focused. Sociable. Dynamic. Optimistic. Enthusiastic.

Attitude: Let's do it differently.

Language:
- Is there another way of doing this?
- That's a great idea!
- Let's try it this way.

Flex your style

The power in understanding the four energy centres comes once you learn how to flex your own style. When we rely only on our own energy preference, we often come up against resistance to our message from those with a different default centre. The trick is learning to move elegantly between all four. Can you speak directly to your audience rather than expecting them to make the effort to understand your perspective? Listening to people with different energy centres talk to each other can be like listening to people speaking completely different languages. By understanding the model and training yourself to flex between the styles, you ensure that what you say won't get lost in translation.

When engaging with a broad audience, it's a good idea to make sure that there's something for everyone in your message: some clear logic, an indication of the human impact, a feeling of choice and a sense of direc-tion. If you have a good idea of what the audience's preference will be, then you have even more scope to tailor your performance – not in an attempt to deceive but in an attempt to deeply connect. When your audi-ence feels as if you're speaking their language, they're much more likely to buy into what you're asking them to do. It all comes down to trust. If you can show people that you understand the way they see the world, you instantly create a bond.

The power of flexing your energy was really driven home for me a couple of years ago when I was trying to influence the decision of a charity board that I was a member of. I went to the meeting with a proposal that I was convinced was in the best interests of the organisation and was excited to share my ideas. My default energy centre is gut, so my presentation was full of big-picture thinking and delivered with great enthusiasm, storytelling and energy. However, it lacked one major component: detail. One of the other board members was very much a head person, and he immediately challenged my pitch and started to pick holes. My initial reaction was to dismiss his objections as nitpicking, and soon we weren't listening to each other anymore. All my hard work was in jeopardy of being dismissed, and the meeting got heated. I found it impossible to understand why he was being so difficult, and in the end, we left the meeting without a resolution.

Once I'd cooled down, it became obvious that I'd made no attempt to see the situation from his perspective, so I set about reworking my presentation. Before the next meeting, I circulated some more detailed analyses, and when we revisited the proposal, I was quickly able to flex my style and convince the room of the merits of my ideas. My head adversary became an ally, and we were able to get unanimous support for my idea. If only I'd done my homework and considered the other energy centres in the room in advance, I could have saved myself a lot of heartache and effort.

ACT OF COMMUNICATION

• •

CONSIDER YOUR AUDIENCE'S ENERGY

Having an educated guess as to your audience's energy centre increases your ability to flex your communication. The following approaches will heighten your awareness of others and ensure that you have more impact:

Listen for language

Pay attention to the language others are using. What do their words tell you about their energy centre? Head people will talk in terms of logic and process. Heart people will talk about emotions and the human impact. Gut people will talk about options and ideas. Feet people will talk about goals and deadlines.

Map your team

On a blank piece of paper, map the energy centres of your team. Write each person's name down and then write 'head', 'heart', 'gut' or 'feet' next to it. What is the dynamic like? Is there a good balance of all four energies? The most effective teams have all four bases covered. Whom do you have the most difficulty communicating with? Do they have a different energy centre than you? If you have a good relationship with everyone, it's worth asking if they agree with your assessment.

In our team at In Flow, each of us lets everyone know what our default centre is and how we like to be communicated with. As I've said, I'm a gut person, and I prefer face-to-face conversations to email. I also prefer to solve problems in the afternoon, as I reserve the mornings to work on important projects. The team knows this, so we schedule meetings after lunch unless there's an emergency. It's amazing how much more productive this simple exercise has made us.

Choose your words carefully

Before meetings and presentations, think about the energy dynamic of the audience. Does your argument speak directly to their energy centre? If there's more than one type of energy centre in the room, have you got something for everybody? It's also helpful to think about the written content you use. What's on your slides or in any documentation you'll be sharing? If your audience is predominantly feet, you'll want to keep things snappy and outcome focused. If you're talking to mostly head people, the details will be key and you'll need to justify how you came to your conclusions. Gut people will be looking for the big picture and the story. Heart people will want to understand the why and the human implications. Make sure you choose language that speaks to your audience and their preferences.

• •

• •

 To download a free copy of the In Flow Energy Centres worksheet visit www.inflow.global/resources

• •

Shine the spotlight on others

I see a lot of people focusing on their own performance. It's a common mistake. In high-stakes scenarios and times of stress, they put themselves in the spotlight. They worry about how they're coming across and overanalyse the impact they're having. This creates a vicious cycle of introspection. You become more and more aware of what you're doing and less and less aware of your audience. This means that you walk away from an interaction unable to articulate the effect you've had on those listening to you, as you thought only about yourself. Of course it's important to reflect after the event, but you shouldn't be thinking about your performance in the heat of the moment.

The best performers in all disciplines do the opposite. They place the focus outside of themselves. Great actors don't focus on their performance while they're on stage – they work with every ounce of their being to affect the other person in the scene. Great athletes don't think about how they look while they're running the race – they focus on the goal, on crossing the finish line ahead of the competition. In communication terms, then, our focus should be on those we're trying to impact, not on our own process. Whenever you communicate, you should be shining the spotlight on your audience, not standing in it yourself. When you do this successfully, nerves slip away, your audience feels included and heard, even if the subject matter is challenging, and your ability to flex your style increases, as you get out of your own way. The impact is amazing.

It comes back to the phrase 'leave yourself alone', which I mentioned in the Mindset chapter. Stop getting in your own way. Stop overanalysing and inhibiting your performance. There's time for self-analysis while you rehearse, prepare and debrief, but when you step on stage, whether that stage is in a theatre or a board-room, it's time to be fully present and in the moment reacting to the stimuli you're given, rather than holding on doggedly to some pre-prepared playbook. Your audience is always more important than you are.

ACT OF COMMUNICATION
• •

CHANGE YOUR FOCUS

If you're the sort of person who is derailed by your own self-talk ensure that you practise shining the spotlight on your audience instead of yourself. Make a conscious effort to focus on them and how they are receiving your communication rather than worrying about your own performance. One of the best ways to do this is to focus on eye contact. Make an effort to connect with each person in the room. As I mentioned in the Presence chapter, if you've looked at them long enough to notice their eye colour then you know you have made a connection.

• •

Keep listening

To keep your attention on your audience, focus on the way you listen. There's a big difference between hearing what someone says and actually listening to it. It's too easy to fall into the trap of allowing words to wash over you while you plan and prepare your response. Instead, give yourself time to take everything in before you reply. Listening helps you to be present; it forces you to place your full attention on the person or people you're interacting with. Listening builds trust and connection. Listening allows you to take the heat out of conflict and build consensus.

In the world of acting, listening is a key differentiator between a good and a bad performance. Good actors listen to the other actors on stage and respond in the moment. The words they speak may be fixed, but how they say them is influenced by the stimuli they receive. Bad actors wait to hear their cue and then say their lines, often unaware of what's really going on in the moment. I see this in the business world all the time. In meeting rooms around the globe, people sit waiting to have their say, to vent their frustration, to express their opinion without really listening to the other voices in the room. They're so intent on getting their point across that they're mostly unaware of what else is being said. Instead of a conversation or a dialogue of exploration, what takes place is a series of simultaneous monologues. An overlap of sound but not of ideas. This is death to collaboration, innovation and creativity – ideals that many organisations strive for but few achieve.

If you want to increase your impact and influence, you need to learn to listen and to listen deeply. Don't just listen with your ears – listen with your eyes and heart as well. What clues can you see that might help you understand the subtext of what's being said? Acknowledge your feelings and be open to expressing them. Telling others how a situation is making you feel often provokes a much more honest exploration of the subject.

The best communicators make their audience feel heard. Even if you're giving a presentation and are the only person speaking, can you show your audience that you understand them? Can you articulate their hopes and fears in the words that you choose and the way that you deliver them? As a rule of thumb, try to spend twice as much time listening as you spend talking. It's easy to do in a meeting. For a speech or presentation, you'll need to spend double the amount of time on your research as you spend on your writing. When you adopt this ratio, you ensure that you always speak from a place of respect and understanding, no matter how difficult the subject matter.

Always have a plan

The simplest thing you can do to improve the quality of your conversations is to plan. Most of us just show up. We pick up the phone or walk into the meeting room and hope for the best. The problem with this is that we open ourselves up to the possibility of surprise, and surprise triggers our fight-or-flight response. When this happens, we enter survival mode – we develop tunnel vision so that we can focus on what we need to fight or run away from and we stop being able to see the big picture. The adage 'If you fail to plan, you are planning to fail' is spot on. Of course you can't envisage every eventuality, but if you don't know your destination, how will you know if you've arrived?

The real art of planning is not in deciding your own tactics but in anticipating the performance of the other side. Sports teams spend hours watching footage of their opposition, analysing their approach and trying to predict what they'll do. The best communicators do the same. I encourage my clients to divide their plan into two parts: me and them. I then get them to consider four categories for both themselves and the people they'll be interacting with:

1. Intentions – What does each party want the other to know, feel and do?

2. Red lines – What are the non-negotiables for each party? At what point would each party walk away from the table?

3. Desirables – What are some of the 'nice to haves' for each party? What would sweeten the deal?

4. Energy centres – Which of the In Flow Energy Centres will each party likely rely on?

This level of detail in your planning may seem arduous at first, but when you get used to it, you'll be able to complete your thinking in a matter of minutes. It will make your communication clearer for your audience and will ultimately make you more strategic and effective under pressure. You'll also find it much easier to adapt if circumstances change. It's not just for negotiations or important meetings either. I also encourage clients to plan at this level before they make phone calls or ask colleagues for help. When you take time to try to deeply understand your audience, you set yourself up for success.

ACT OF COMMUNICATION
• •

CREATE YOUR PLANNER

I have a specific template, which we created at In Flow, that I use to prepare for meetings and phone calls. If it works for you, feel free to copy it. If it doesn't, what additional information do you need to think about to make sure you're prepared? Whatever you add, make sure you consider it from both the me perspective and the them perspective. Think about the next conversation you're going to have and fill in the planner:

THE IN FLOW CONVERSATION PLANNER

	Me	Them
Intention: Know?		
Intention: Feel?		
Intention: Do?		
Red lines?		
Desirables?		
In Flow Energy Centres?		
Notes		

To download a free copy of the
In Flow Conversation Planner visit
www.inflow.global/resources

It's not about you

Putting your audience at the heart of your communication instantly increases your influence. Whether you find yourself in a conflict situation or trying to get buy-in for a new idea, the more you know about your audience, the more you can tailor your performance to meet their needs. You'll get your outcome, but they'll feel as if they've won too.

I'll always remember how Jonathan Frakes, the director of *Thunderbirds*, used to get everyone ready to film an important scene. Before he became a movie director, Jonathan had a high-profile career as an actor (most famously, he played the character of Riker in the *Star Trek* franchise). Jonathan understood his cast. He knew what it was like to be in a big-budget movie where simple mistakes could cost thousands of dollars in lost time. He knew how stressful it could be walking onto set, and he knew that a state of fight-or-flight was not a good place for his cast to be in. To combat this, he did something simple. He sang. Jonathan set himself up with a microphone and a PA system, and whenever we walked onto set, he would serenade us with a silly song and crack light-hearted jokes. This instantly made the tension of the moment melt away and ensured that we were relaxed in front of the camera. It was a brilliant piece of influencing and leadership. He understood his audience, and he made sure he got the performance he wanted by stepping into our shoes and seeing the situation from our perspective.

Next time you find yourself in a high-stakes situation, ask yourself what you can do to make sure that you place your audience centre stage. Find out as much about them as you can in advance. Notice the energy that they bring to the situation. Put the spotlight firmly on them. Listen to what they say in the moment. Have a clear plan and remain open and flexible enough to deviate from it. If you do all that, you can't fail to make an impact.

Chapter Five

CONTENT

Understand the magic of words

One of the biggest challenges in communication is knowing exactly what to say. I'm sure you've been in a situation where you've been lost for words, where you've found it difficult to articulate your thoughts. It happens to all of us. Even when we know our subject matter inside out, we can still struggle to find the right language to bring our ideas to life. And if we choose the wrong words, we make our lives even harder. How often has your message been misinterpreted or your meaning misconstrued? If we pick the wrong combinations of letters, we can quickly find ourselves in trouble.

Words have magic powers. They compel us to do things. They stir emotion. They can fire us up or freeze us to the spot. A simple yes can start an unstoppable chain of events and a simple no can slam on the brakes and create an immovable impasse. We must therefore choose our words wisely. In an era of instant information, we're used to consuming content at a phenomenal pace. While most of us read fewer books than our parents and grandparents, we see many more words. And as we move out of the industrial age into the ideas economy, we spend more time talking and listening than we spend doing. Think of the volume of emails you receive. The number of social media posts you scroll through. The barrage of blogs and articles you consume. The meetings you attend. The videos you watch. The conference calls and message threads you participate in. As consumers of words, we tend to engage at a superficial level, scanning for what is immediately interesting and relevant, discarding what is not. We rarely pause to deeply consider the language we're seeing or hearing. It washes over us in waves.

As communicators, as producers of content, we need to be aware of this paradox. Our audience is swimming in words, yet they largely remain untouched by them. If we want our words to go past their eyes and ears and reach their minds and hearts, we need to be conscious of the language that we choose. We need to craft our messages for maximum impact and ensure that our ideas stand out from the crowd. We need to stop talking in acronyms and 'business speak' and start treating our audiences like the human beings they are. When we take time to choose our words, whether written or spoken, we can move people. We don't have to be poetic or flowery – we just need to craft our message to suit the situation and the people on the receiving end.

Speak to the imagination

They say a picture paints a thousand words. Your job as a communicator is to use your words to paint pictures in the minds of your audiences. The human imagination is infinitely powerful. What we can imagine we can create. Every single human-made thing is the product of someone's imagination. The keyboard I'm typing on, the chair I'm sitting on, the jumper I'm wearing – all these things were brought into being because someone imagined them. Human beings cannot create without first imagining, so if we want our audience to act upon our words, we have to help them imagine the outcome we want to achieve.

The best content speaks to people's imaginations. It allows them to visualise what we're talking about and create their own representations of our message. The human brain finds it difficult to distinguish between what is real and what is imagined. Think about your favourite food. Picture it in front of you in as much detail as possible. What does it look like? What colours do you see? What texture is it? How does it smell? Imagine you were just about to eat a delicious mouthful… Have you started to salivate yet? This simple act of imagining is enough to get most people's brains to start producing the enzymes necessary to digest the real thing. That means that if we can get people to imagine what we're talking about, we're halfway towards turning it into reality.

Use structure to give you freedom

For many of us, creativity is daunting. We stare at a blank piece of paper or an empty document on our computer screen and agonise about where to start. What if we get it wrong? What if it doesn't make sense? What if the right words don't come? We look at others who seem comfortable with uncertainty and speaking off the cuff and think that we can never achieve that level of relaxation and freedom. How are some people able to get their message across with ease while others stumble and stall? The secret lies in understanding the art of improvisation. To the outside eye, an actor who is improvising seems to be in free fall with no safety net to protect them. The reality couldn't be further from the truth.

When I arrived at drama school, the idea of improvisation filled me with dread. I remember sitting in my first improv class feeling sick to my stomach at the prospect of being picked to do an exercise in front of my peers. I felt out of control and vulnerable. It took me over a year to learn a secret that would transform me from someone who hated this kind of spontaneity to someone who relished it. The secret is that improvisation isn't about uncertainty – it's about structure. Without a clear set of rules for the performer, everything falls apart. The more detailed and defined the rules, the more freedom you have. When great actors improvise, they agree to the rules of the game in advance. They may be finding the words in that moment, but they can rely on each other to respect the structure and not deviate from it. The result is a seemingly effortless performance that leaves the audience enthralled.

Rather than getting the people I work with to think of their content as scripts that they need to learn off by heart, I encourage them to clearly define the structure and then improvise inside the framework. Actors find it difficult enough to learn lines, and they get paid for it. You shouldn't be committing business presentations to memory or trying to give word-perfect feedback to your direct reports. All that does is make you focus on remembering what to say at the expense of being present with your audience. Instead, find the right structure for your message and then give yourself permission to experiment and find your flow. This will allow you the freedom to improvise, safe in the knowledge that your message is supported by rock-solid scaffolding that's invisible to your audience. You'll know it's there in the background, but the people on the receiving end will be blissfully unaware and will focus only on the power of your words.

In this chapter, I'm going to share four of the content for-mulas I've developed for my clients. They're designed to be aide-memoires that help you to structure your thinking before you go into difficult situations and to react effortlessly in the moment should you find yourself on the spot. There are four key areas where people seem to struggle to find the right words:

1. Starting presentations

2. Telling stories

3. Networking introductions

4. Giving feedback

The formulas on the pages that follow address each of these problem areas in turn. Even if you don't find yourself in these situations often, I suggest you work through them one by one, so that you have a strategy should you find yourself stuck in the future. Once they become familiar, you'll also begin to see opportunities to deploy each formula in multiple situations. Think of them as your secret weapons for ensuring that your words have more impact.

Starting presentations: begin with a bang

The latest research suggests that it takes somewhere between 33 and 100 microseconds to form a first impression. Whatever the actual number, it doesn't take long, and our audiences' attention spans are only getting shorter. We've conditioned ourselves to swipe, scroll and switch in an instant if something doesn't capture our imagination. Distractions abound, so you have to accept the reality that your audience isn't necessarily focused on the task at hand. Be honest with yourself. Have you ever checked your emails while on a conference call? Have you ever scrolled through your phone for messages during a meeting? Have you ever browsed the internet while someone gave a presentation? If you haven't done at least one of the three, you're in the miniscule minority. For better or worse (and in my opinion, definitely for worse), multitasking has become the norm. We're constantly competing for our audience's attention and if we don't grab it from the outset, we risk losing it altogether.

Cast your mind back over the last ten presentations you sat through. How many captured your attention from the word go? In my experience, most presenters ease their audience in. They start with some empty platitudes and a predictable list of housekeeping items that are forgettable at best. They then proceed to walk everyone through a bland agenda and only get to the important stuff way after the clock has passed the sixty-second mark. They have failed to make a strong first impression and as a result have made it extremely difficult for their audience to focus on their message. If you want to make an impact, begin with a bang. You don't have to pull a rabbit out of a hat, but I do recommend starting your interactions in a way that makes people sit up and pay attention.

If you're anything like me, you're probably most nervous during the first couple of minutes of giving a presentation.

There's normally a lot at stake in these moments, which is why it's tempting to play it safe and start gently. It might work for you, but it won't work for your audience. You need to start strong. I know that once I've got through the opening and am into my flow, I'll naturally start to relax, so I've created a formula to ensure I have a foolproof beginning to any presentation. Now I can craft my opening in a matter of seconds, knowing that it will grab my audience's attention and make them curious about what's to come. I call it a STAR opening.

STAR stands for Surprise, Takeaways, Authority and Roadmap. Let's explore each element in more detail.

Start with a surprise

Kick off with something different. A fact. A statistic. A quote. A story. A controversial statement. An image. A video. A joke. Something that changes the energy in the room. It doesn't have to be mind-blowing – just an alternative to the opening statements they're used to hearing. When you begin in this way, you'll be amazed at how quickly people put their phones down, close their laptops, sit up and start listening.

Tell them the takeaways

What's in it for the audience? You need to put them at ease. Most people start from the premise 'What's in it for me?' They're sitting there wondering, 'Is this relevant or a complete waste of my time?' You need to hit those objections head-on. Tell them what they stand to gain from listening to you, and you'll start to build curiosity.

Articulate your authority

Now that they're listening and you've got them relaxed, it's time to tell them who you are and why they should listen to you. What makes you credible? Why are you the right person to be talking about this topic? Many people start with this sort of information, but doing so can instantly switch the audience off. People will be much more open to finding out about you after hearing the takeaways, and you'll begin to create trust. If you're already known to your audience, obviously it would be odd to say your name or announce your job title at this point. Instead, use your authority statement to give them some facts they don't already know about you or to tell them why you, specifically, are talking about this topic.

Reveal the roadmap

People want to know what's in store. This is your opportunity to give them a 30,000-foot view of where you're going with them during the session. Let them have an outline but don't give it all away! The roadmap could be your agenda or information about how you're planning to structure the presentation or meeting. Don't confuse the roadmap with the takeaways. The roadmap is simply a list of the steps you're going to take together, not the highlights. You're now ready to move into the body of the presentation or meeting.

What I like about the STAR opening is how flexible and invisible it is. I use it as a structure for the beginning of pretty much every presentation and training session I run, and unless you've read this book or have been on one of our courses, I can guarantee you'd never know. Sometimes I'll choose a sentence for each section and sometimes the whole thing can last ten minutes. It just depends on the audience, the circumstances and how much time is available. By following the four steps, you'll be able to create a unique and compelling opening that will leave your audience wanting more. And I'd encourage you to think of this as more than just a way of starting presentations. Consider deploying it in meetings and on phone calls as well, to ensure that you make a strong and lasting impression.

• •

 To watch my video about creating a STAR opening, visit www.inflow.global/star

• •

ACT OF COMMUNICATION

• •

CREATE A STAR OPENING

Next time you're planning a presentation or thinking about how to kick off a meeting, use the STAR formula to create your opening. With practice, you'll be able to outline what you're going to say in a matter of minutes. Once you've decided on an appropriate *surprise*, jot down a couple of bullet points to outline the key *takeaways* for the audience. You shouldn't have to think much about your *authority*, as you know what you've achieved. My only advice is to not be too modest. It's important that your audience trusts that you know what you're talking about, so don't be afraid to talk about your achievements. Finally, sketch out the *roadmap*. What will you be covering during the presentation or meeting? Three to five high-level topics are more than enough. Will you be using one of the frames we covered in the Mindset chapter? If so, it's useful to position that here too. Then it's time to practise. It's important to always practise speaking your words aloud and not to over-script things. The more you use the formula, the easier and more instinctive it will become.

• •

Telling stories: take them on a journey

Take a look at the front of any newspaper and you'll see the adage 'Facts tell; stories sell' in action. An evocative headline usually has fewer than seven words and gets straight to the heart of the story. You won't find a spreadsheet, a graph, or 2,000 words of analysis. The reason for this is that human beings are hardwired for stories. Since the beginning of civilisation, we've been using stories to teach the difference between right and wrong, to share our successes and failures, and to warn each other of danger. When we hear a story, our bodies produce oxytocin, the social-bonding hormone, and we start to build trust with the person we're listening to. Stories bind us together and help us make sense of the world.

If you want to capture people's imaginations and make more of an impact, you need to build your storytelling muscles. It's easy in the world of business to focus on the data, to lead with the numbers and ignore the narrative underneath. And yet, each spreadsheet and graph tells a story which, once articulated, allows the audience to connect the numbers to something more human. The details are important, but too many of them and people can't see the wood for the trees. Think about your content and your message – What's the underlying story you want to tell? What imaginative journey do you want to take people on? Don't think about the story as childish or as dumbing down your message. Instead, think about it as a way of bringing your content into full colour, sharply focused, high definition. Stories allow you to illuminate your subject matter and bring it to life in the hearts and minds of your audience.

Storytelling is a great way to illustrate an idea. By telling a story, you help the audience put themselves at the heart of your narrative, making them more open to acting upon that idea. Stories and metaphors are used by every religion and in every educational institution on the planet as a way of imparting knowledge and wisdom. Think about how you could use stories in your meetings, calls and presentations to make your content more interesting and appealing. The SELL formula is an effective way to maximise the impact of a story.

SELL stands for Setting, Event, Link and Learning. Let's look at each part in turn.

Setting

What's the context of the story? Set the scene in as much detail as possible so that your audience can picture exactly what you're talking about. What did it look like? What did it sound like? What did it smell like? Use sensory language to paint a vivid picture for your audience.

Event

What's the turning point in the story? What event occurred that caused a change? What's the climax of the story? This can be a moment of realisation, the discovery of a solution, or the point when everything went wrong. The event is the key moment in the story's arc – the moment you want the audience to focus on.

Link

This is where you make your connection to the story clear. How did the situation impact you personally? What emotion did the event create? It's important to talk from an 'I' perspective at this point (e.g. 'I felt proud/ excited/disappointed'). If you're telling the story from someone else's point of view, convey how they felt when the event occurred.

Learning

What lesson do you want your audience to take away? Why was it important to share this story? This is your opportunity to make your message land and to drive home the point you've used the story to illustrate. Sometimes you might choose not to reveal the learning, to allow the audience to draw their own conclusions. This can be powerful in a teaching situation.

The SELL formula keeps your storytelling on track and stops you from rambling or going around the houses. It's an intuitive way to deliver a narrative and makes it easy for your audience to follow. Whether you're telling your personal story or sharing a business case study, it's important that your story flows and takes your audience on a journey.

When I set up my training company, my instinct was to hide my personal story from our clients. Despite the fact that I'd done some things I was immensely proud of as an actor, I thought that if I wanted to be taken seriously in the world of business, I needed to project a more polished corporate image. One rainy November day, I found myself sitting in a small, dull office in Northern England sipping tea with my business coach. In Flow was a couple of months old but it was struggling to find its identity and we weren't making money.

Out of the blue my coach asked me a question that changed everything. 'Why don't any of your marketing materials mention your past? Aren't you proud of it?'

'Of course I'm proud of it,' I replied. 'It just isn't relevant.'

The second those words left my mouth, I realised my mistake. By failing to share my previous experiences, I was changing my story from something interesting and unique into something bland and vanilla. The drama had disappeared and the narrative I was presenting had become boring. In an attempt to fit in, I had lost my sense of identity.

I see it all the time with my clients. A reluctance to share stories for fear of appearing either boring or boastful. But our stories are what make us unique. I'm not encouraging you to show off or regale people with a list of your every accomplishment. I'm advocating sharing things about yourself that help you connect with your audience. We don't read the CVs of those we admire – we read their biographies. We want to glimpse behind the curtain. To experience the highs and lows. Stories help your audience do just that. I encourage you to share them whenever the opportunity arises.

In case you didn't spot it, if you'd like an example of the SELL formula in action, reread the story above.

ACT OF COMMUNICATION

• •

SELL YOUR IDEA

Think about the next meeting, presentation or phone call you have. Is there an opportunity to tell a story? Is there a concept or idea that would benefit from being illustrated in a more creative way? Take a blank piece of paper and fold it in half, then in half again. Open it out and you should have four boxes marked with fold lines. Now write one of the following headings in each of the four boxes: Setting, Event, Link and Learning. Think of a true story that would bring your message to life. Use the four quadrants to plan your story using bullet points. You don't need to write a script – you're describing something that has already happened, so you can't get it wrong. Try this out at the next opportunity and see how much more engaged your audience is with your topic.

• •

Networking introductions: create curiosity

A big advantage of storytelling is that it instantly makes you more interesting and memorable. If you've ever been to a networking event, you'll know how painful introductions can be. I'll always remember going to a business breakfast shortly after setting up my training company and feeling as though I wanted the ground to swallow me up. As I've mentioned, I'm a natural introvert, so having to converse with a roomful of strangers isn't my idea of fun. And to make matters worse, I'd just read an article about the importance of having a strong elevator pitch. While driving to the venue, I crafted and rehearsed my thirty-second spiel about what I did and whom I helped. Unfortunately, when I deployed it in the room, it fell on deaf ears. As soon as I mentioned the word 'training', there was one of those awkward tumbleweed moments. It seemed as if no one was interested in who I was or what I had to offer. I left the room vowing never to use an elevator pitch again. But what was I going to do instead? How could I introduce myself in an interesting way and, most importantly, open up a conversation?

After a little bit of trial and error, I arrived at the perfect formula. Now, whenever I have to introduce myself to strangers, I use Past, Present, Future to kick off the conversation.

Past

Let your audience know something interesting or unexpected about your past. Where else have you worked? What have you been doing recently that's unusual or memorable? Tell them something about yourself that stands out, rather than just reciting a bland job title.

Present

Help the audience to get clarity about your present situation. What are you doing now? What are you working on at the moment that's exciting, interesting or challenging? Create a compelling image of where you are currently.

Future

Tell your audience about your plans. What's going to happen in the next few weeks? What's just around the corner? What do you hope to achieve in the next year or even the next five years? Encourage your audience to imagine what the future might look like.

The great thing about this formula is that it allows you to create a snappy twenty-second intro (one or two sentences for each section), or you can flesh things out and use a five-minute version if you need to go into more detail. Now when someone asks the dreaded question 'What do you do?' I reply with something like 'I actually started my career as an actor, and my claim to fame is playing Virgil Tracy in the 2004 Hollywood remake of *Thunderbirds* with Sir Ben Kingsley and Bill Paxton. I now run a company called In Flow, and we specialise in sharing the skills I learned on stage and screen to help business people speak and perform under pressure. Next month I'm going to be in the US working with the board of a multinational on how to communicate their change agenda to the organisation. How about you?'

What I love about this response is that it gives my audience choice. If the acting side of things interests them, we can talk about that. If they have questions about our training methods, the conversation can naturally go in that direction. Or if their Auntie Sue lives in Houston, Texas, we can have a natter about cornbread and country music. Whatever way the conversation goes, we can find common ground and start to build rapport.

Past, Present, Future is an act of generosity and should help you avoid those awkward silences whenever you introduce yourself. It's also a brilliant framework for updating others on the progress of a project or to highlight a series of achievements. I regularly use it in client meetings and presentations, and I encourage those I coach to do the same. Talk about how things used to be, where you are now and how the future will look. Just like the SELL formula, it has a clear beginning, middle and end, which provides vital structure to your communication. It allows your audience to understand where they are in the narrative and to navigate themselves through your material. Every presentation, meeting and phone call naturally has these three elements, but great communicators make them explicit and allow them to land.

ACT OF COMMUNICATION
• •

NETWORK GENEROUSLY

Before you attend your next networking event or enter a situation where you'll be meeting new people, plan a Past, Present, Future introduction. You might think there's nothing particularly interesting about your life, but that's simply not true. Each person's life is made up of a unique set of experiences. No one else has walked exactly the same path as you have. You are one of a kind, and there will never be another you on the planet. Sharing something about yourself with others shows people that you're willing to let your guard down and give them a glimpse into your world. You don't have to reveal all the skeletons in your closet. Just give them a flavour of who you are and what you have achieved. It's a good idea to finish your introduction with an open question, to help stimulate the conversation.

• •

• •

 I'm so passionate about the idea of people sharing their stories that I made Past, Present, Future the basis of a TEDx talk I did in Vitoria-Gasteiz, Spain, in 2017. You can watch the video at www.inflow.global/TED

• •

Giving feedback: be honest and fearless

No matter what your level of experience, one of the most challenging types of communication is the act of giving feedback. We tend to prefer to keep emotion outside of the workplace, and nothing has more potential to make things bubble to the surface than a bit of constructive criticism. In most feedback situations, both the giver and the receiver are on edge, hoping not to provoke an unwanted reaction. Both parties can end up being defensive, and the intended message often fails to land. Being able to give an honest assessment of a situation or another person's performance is a vital tool in your communication-skills toolkit. There are four principles I suggest you adhere to – think of them as an ABCD for fearless feedback.

Accurate

Ensure that your comments are specific, not generalised. 'That was great' or 'I didn't like what you did then' doesn't tell the person anything. What specifically was great? How could they improve? It's useful to describe your observations in as much detail as possible so that the listener can pinpoint exactly what the feedback pertains to.

Behavioural

The best feedback focuses on behaviour. You might not be able to instantly change outcomes, but you can instantly change how you behave. Describing the behaviour or the events you have observed helps others to think about what they can do differently in the future. When you give feedback in this way, it immediately becomes actionable.

Constructive

Being constructive isn't about being touchy-feely or nice. It's about knowing why you're giving the feedback in the first place. Is it about helping the other party to improve? Or do you just want to get your feelings off your chest? If it's the latter, think twice about opening your mouth. I'd also suggest avoiding the common technique of sandwiching a piece of constructive feedback between two positive comments. Most people can see this coming a mile off, and the perceived negative cancels out the positive, which means that the good stuff doesn't get heard. Own your feedback and don't be afraid to be direct.

Dialogue

Be wary of giving a lecture – sometimes receiving feedback can make us feel like a naughty child being told off. Instead, aim to have a performance dialogue.

You and the other person need to agree on what the problem is and find a solution for how to move forward. If you don't, you're unlikely to see a change in behaviour, and resentment can develop quickly. Look for opportunities to ask open questions and to allow the other person to speak. It might feel uncomfortable, but it's much more effective than a monologue that falls on deaf ears.

A useful acronym for structuring difficult feedback is EPIC. This framework allows you to name your emotions without getting emotional, which means you can remain assertive when the stakes are high. It's equally effective when speaking one-to-one or when requesting a change in behaviour from a large group.

Evidence

Describe the behaviour or situation as completely and objectively as possible. What evidence do you have? Avoid accusations or value judgements. Use only the facts!

Position

Express your feelings and thoughts about the behaviour or situation. Explain the position you find yourself in. How do you feel? What does the situation look like from your perspective? Phrase your statements using 'I' not 'you'.

Ideal

Specify the ideal behaviour or outcome. What would good look like? How could the situation be improved? Make sure the other party knows exactly what you expect and how it can be achieved.

Consequences

State the consequences. It's useful to think about them in both positive and negative terms. What will happen if a change in behaviour occurs? What will happen if it doesn't?

Let's look at an example. Imagine that someone on your team is continually turning up later than everyone else. It's starting to damage morale and you want to bring it up as part of an appraisal. The reality is that you're unlikely to be able to sit down with someone and run through the EPIC framework without inter-ruption. It's much more likely to be part of a conversation. The great thing about the framework is it keeps you on track and stops the conversation from turning into an emotional conflict.

Your first job is to present the evidence. What are the facts? How many times have they been late in the last month? What time did they get in each day this week? What does it say in their contract about working hours? It's important at this stage that you get agreement around the evidence. Allow the other person to state the facts from their perspective until you come to a consensus, but don't allow any justification or reasoning at this stage.

The second step is to present your position. How do you feel about what's going on? Frustrated? Disappointed? Annoyed? Talk about your feelings or those of the team but avoid apportioning blame. 'I feel really annoyed' will be received very differently by the other party than 'What you're doing is really annoying me'. No one can dispute your emotions, so don't be afraid to state them. Often when the other party hears this part of the framework it's a big shock, as they never intended to make other people feel something negative.

The next thing to do is to state your ideal. What do you want the other party to agree to? What outcome are you looking for? How will they know that they've achieved success? Perhaps you want them to agree to always being at their desk by 9am or to commit to emailing the team in advance if they're going to be late. It's important that you're in the driving seat of this part of the conversation. This is where you can be assertive. Your ideal must be an unambiguous, direct request.

The final thing to do is to highlight the consequences. If they change their behaviour, how will it affect the team dynamic? How will it impact productivity and their chances of promotion? Equally, if they don't achieve your ideal, what will happen? Does it become a more formal disciplinary matter? Will HR have to get involved? It's worth putting forward both the positive and negative consequences, as doing so will allow the other party to understand the full implications of the choice they decide to make.

Your job when giving feedback is to keep coming back to the EPIC framework. The other party will inevitably go off track, so bring them back. If you walk through the steps in order, it will stop the conversation from becoming emotional. You'll have an opportunity to discuss the emotional impact of the behaviour without entering into conflict. This is a great way to make difficult conversations smoother and more impactful.

ACT OF COMMUNICATION

● ●

HAVE COURAGEOUS CONVERSATIONS

Take a moment to think about some feedback that you'd like to give someone. It doesn't have to be something of great significance. In fact, it's often easier to practise using the EPIC framework in a low-stakes environment. It works just as well for delivering positive feedback too! Write the acronym EPIC on a sticky note and jot down two or three bullet points for each letter. When you're having the feedback conversation, refer to your sticky note and use it to keep things on track. Make sure you go through the feedback step by step and notice what impact it has on the emotional tone of the interaction. If you do it right, the conversation will be open and constructive.

● ●

Forget everything you've planned

The structures I've just shared are designed to give you confidence. They'll help you prepare yourself to communicate at your best in high-pressure situations. But I want to say one final thing about content: as soon as you get in front of your audience, be prepared to forget everything you've planned. This might seem like a contradiction, given that I've dedicated so much of the chapter to frameworks and formulas. However, there is no right or wrong. Your audience can't mind-read and they don't have a clue what's going to come out of your mouth. Structure is there as a guide, but there's no substitute for human connection. Prepare and then forget about your preparation and concentrate on who's in front of you. Trust that you'll find the right words. Focus on being in the moment. If you've got clear intentions, you've entered into the right mindset, you're working on being present, you understand your audience, and you've done your homework, your content will take care of itself.

Chapter Six

TECHNIQUE

Be more you

It's easy when reading a book like this to feel that the tools and techniques are outside your grasp, that you need to transform into someone else in order to succeed. The reality couldn't be further from the truth. I'm not interested in turning you into a perfect communicator – some sort of robot who always makes the same choice. Your uniqueness is your strength. You need to become more you, not less. You do that by building your technique. Think of anyone who's a top performer in their field; they have their own way of doing things, and that's part of what makes them stand out. Underpinning everything they do is a core set of principles and behaviours that they've developed and refined. What elements of your communication do you need to work on most? What skills would you like to develop?

Technique is about doing the work. It's about taking what you've learned in the previous chapters and making it your own. The fact that you've read this far, that you haven't given up and put the book back on the shelf, tells me that you have the determination and character to succeed. You've taken the first step. You've begun the process of change. That process happens over time. There is no overnight transformation. Of course there are some quick wins to be had, but the exciting growth happens more slowly, as you start to bring all the elements together. You need to build the muscles and continue to experiment to find out what works for you.

When learning any new skill, there's always a period of discomfort. You have to be prepared to make mistakes, but you don't need to start from scratch. You've been communicating since the moment you were born. You just need to work out what needs turning up and what needs turning down. As discussed, we all show different sides of ourselves in different contexts. I behave in one way when I'm at home with my family and in another when I'm giving a keynote speech at a sales conference. I bring a different sort of energy to each environment. I'm not pretending or trying to manipulate my audience – I'm just allowing different parts of my personality to come through. When we heighten our awareness of the range we have available to us, we become more dynamic. Start to notice the various versions of yourself and then explore using them in other situations. The more freedom and choice you find in your performance, the more authentic you become.

Create new habits

The most effective way to grow is to develop new habits. Think 'little' and 'often'. Decide what you're going to focus on and then do something to work towards it every single day. When I arrived at drama school, I didn't like my voice. I didn't have great breath control and the sound was quite tight and not very resonant. I had no experience with vocal training, but I was willing to learn. We had voice classes three times a week, and once I'd learned the exercises, I started doing them each morning as part of my own routine. Over time it became second nature. Vocal warm-ups became as much a part of my day as brushing my teeth or having a shower. Now I do them on autopilot before a training session or a speech. I'll often hum along to the radio or do some articulation exercises in the car without really thinking about it. They've become habits which take care of themselves.

Developing a new skill set can be daunting. We live busy lives, and the thought of adding more to our schedule can make us feel overwhelmed. For this reason, I advocate a technique known as habit chaining. Rather than trying to insert lots of new activity into your day, look for something you already do regularly and attach the new behaviour you want to practise to it. For example, link stretching to getting dressed, or two minutes of deep breathing to the beginning of your drive to work. The more mundane and low stakes the environments you choose, the better. Work on your posture while you sit at your desk checking your emails. Practise your articulation and the power of the pause as you order your morning coffee. The more you build the habit and the muscle, the more likely the behaviour will kick in when you need it.

ACT OF COMMUNICATION

• •

MAKE A SMALL CHANGE

Which area of your performance would benefit the most from a stronger technique? Do you need to work on your physical presence? Or would having a clearer emotional intention get you better results? Once you've identified the area that you want to work on, look for a current habit that you could chain the new behaviour to. Take a blank piece of paper and a pencil and draw a twenty-eight-box grid – four columns, seven rows. Stick the paper somewhere prominent so that you see it every day. Don't label it or tell other people what it is. This is about showing yourself what you're capable of, not showing other people what you're doing. For the next twenty-eight days, simply cross off a box when you perform your new habit. Once you've crossed off a couple of boxes, the visual cue will help you stay on track, and you won't want to break the chain. After you hit the target, choose a new area to work on and repeat the process.

HABIT GRID

To download a free version of the habit grid visit www.inflow.global/resources

Rehearse out loud

The importance of rehearsal cannot be underestimated. It's fundamental to creating a world-class performance. Without it, you risk embarrassing yourself in front of your audience. In the world of theatre, actors normally spend between four and six weeks rehearsing a play before they perform it in front of a paying public. All those hours of private practice finally lead to a performance that looks effortless – one that makes the audience believe that the characters are speaking the words for the first time. The same is true in the world of business. If you want to create a good impression, and if you want to be able to make an impact and influence others, you have to rehearse. You have to practise before you can really find your flow.

Early in my career, I was working on a play in which, for a number of reasons, my scenes had been under-rehearsed. As we neared opening night, it became clear to me that the director had other priorities and, despite my numerous requests, we wouldn't get enough time to work on my parts of the show. I knew how important that rehearsal time was and that if I didn't get it,

I risked delivering a subpar performance and attracting poor reviews. It was a risk I wasn't prepared to take. I gave the director and producer an ultimatum. Unless they found time to work on my scenes, I would walk away from the production. It wasn't a decision I made lightly, but I had to protect my professional reputation. Thankfully, after some productive discussions, the creative team acknowledged the issue and some time was put aside to finesse the scenes. The show was a huge success and received rave reviews. Finding time to rehearse paid off and everyone, especially the audience, benefited as a result. I suggest that you protect your rehearsal time at all costs. Put it in your diary and don't allow others to steal or interrupt it. You'll feel much more confident and will give a better performance if you do.

It's important to distinguish between mental rehearsal and physical rehearsal. While mental rehearsal has some benefits, there's no substitute for speaking the words out loud and doing the actions. If mental rehearsal alone produced brilliant performances, theatre producers around the globe would save themselves a fortune by sending the cast the script and telling them to turn up on opening night. Instead, they invest heavily in bringing the cast together in advance because they know that if they didn't, the results would be catastrophic. The actors might manage to learn their lines, but they would be doing everything in isolation. They wouldn't know where to stand. They wouldn't know how the other actors were going to give them their cues. There would be no chemistry, and the performances would fall flat.

Physical rehearsal is about building muscle memory so that your body knows what it's like to say the words. Even if you're not learning a script, the act of articulating your thoughts, out loud, in advance, means that you'll be able to find the right thing to say when the moment comes. So many business people think that mental rehearsal is enough, that a few minutes spent reviewing the PowerPoint will miraculously enable them to bring the message to life when the meeting begins. Unfortunately, this isn't the case. I'm sure that you've sat through more boring presentations than you care to remember. In most instances, if the presenter had bothered to take time to speak the words aloud in advance, they would have realised how boring they were being and changed their performance accordingly. Proper rehearsal takes effort, but the payoff is worth it.

Finally, remember that rehearsal isn't just something you need to do for presentations or speeches. You should be rehearsing before phone calls, meetings and one-to-ones too. Get used to getting your mouth around the words. Get the experience into your body. If you plan on standing up during the real thing, stand up. If you plan to have props, rehearse with them. If you plan to draw a diagram, draw it in rehearsal. If you're going to use a clicker, have it in your hand. For particularly tricky meetings or one-to-one situations, you may want to ask a friend or colleague to role-play with you. While doing this can feel a bit naff or fake as you practise, I promise that you'll be thankful you did when it's time to do it for real. In our Accelerator Programme, one of the modules has a role-play element, and we bring in a professional actor to work with the delegates. People always say that it's the part of the training they're dreading the most, but afterwards, they're amazed by how beneficial the experience was. The more you rehearse, the more effortless your performance will look. Your audience doesn't want to see the work, so make sure you do the work in advance.

Take it one step at a time

Hopefully by now you have lots of ideas about things you want to try and tools you want to practise with. As desperate as you may be to make some changes, here are some words of warning: don't try to do it all at once. You don't learn to juggle six balls by picking up all six and tossing them in the air until it clicks. Instead, you start with one. Once you've mastered that, you add a second, and then a third, building yourself up one step at a time. When people work on their communication, they often try to change everything at once. It's a sure-fire route to failure and will leave you feeling frustrated and demotivated. I recommend an approach that I first developed when working as a theatre director. I noticed that after I gave the cast feedback during notes sessions, the actors would try to incorporate all the changes I'd asked for into the next performance. This only made things worse. To remedy this, I started asking them to focus on just one thing that they wanted to work on in the next show – to have a single focus and let everything else take care of itself. The results were extraordinary. The thing they were working on inevitably improved, but so did lots of other things. I'd ask you to do the same as you build your technique. Don't try to change everything. Identify a key thing that you'd like to improve and focus only on that. Once you feel you've mastered it, then, and only then, move on to the next thing on your list.

Warm up

Actors warm up. Athletes warm up. Most people in business don't. If you want to give the best possible performance, make sure you're prepped and ready to go. When you break it down, warming up has two outcomes: it gets you physically ready and it gets you mentally ready. As we explored in the Mindset chapter, the mind-body link is incredibly powerful, so a physical warm-up is a big part of getting us in the zone. Visit any theatre in the land this evening and backstage, thirty minutes before the curtain goes up, you'll find the cast stretching, humming and getting focused on the task at hand. It's a standard part of the actor's toolkit, and I recommend making it part of your communication toolkit too.

I also suggest that you split every warm-up into three parts: body, voice and mind. Think of each part as a separate muscle that needs to be gently stretched and manipulated to ensure that it works at its best.

Body

We start with the body because if the body is tense, the voice and mind will be too. Relaxation is infectious. When we start to free the body, we create a ripple of energy that we can turn into a powerful wave on which to carry our message. Focus on the shoulders and neck and then release any other areas where you're holding tension. Work for freedom of movement. Feel the weight in the limbs. Don't forget to relax the jaw and the muscles of the face, too, so that you can clearly articulate your ideas.

Voice

Once the body is warmed up, move on to the voice. As we've discussed, warming up your speaking instrument is especially important first thing in the morning. Over the course of the day, after you've spent some time speaking, the voice naturally becomes more relaxed and resonant. It's always good to deepen this relaxation, but if your important meeting, phone call or presentation is at 8.30am, warming up is essential. You need to make sure you're ready. Do some of the humming exercises I suggested in the Presence chapter, to give your voice more resonance and gravitas. It's also worth playing around with pitch, to give the voice more colour, and stretching the muscles of articulation, to give you more clarity. Working on these areas for just a couple of minutes before you speak will give you much more vocal impact and will help you land your message.

Mind

Finally, focus on the mind. Is your intention clear? Have you taken control of your mindset? I always finish my warm-up with a couple of minutes of deep breathing. This doesn't have to be done lying on the floor or sitting in a chair. You can focus on your breath as you walk down the corridor or sit in a meeting room waiting for everyone to arrive. As we explored in the Mindset chapter, diaphragmatic breathing helps to reduce your threat response and gets you ready to perform.

There is no substitute for an effective warm-up. Make time to do it and you make time to succeed.

ACT OF COMMUNICATION

• •

CHOREOGRAPH A ROUTINE

You need to own your warm-up routine. The Head, Shoulders, Knees and Toes exercise in the Presence chapter is a great reference point, but it's important to identify your own needs and put some steps in place to address them. Spend five minutes planning your personal warm-up.

What elements should it include? Where do you habitually hold physical tension? Make sure you relax that area of the body. What aspects of your vocal presence do you need to address most? Make sure there's something in your routine that deals with that. What do you need to do to calm the voices in your head? Put that into the mix too. It's also worth creating routines of different lengths. I have a ninety-second rapid-fire routine, a ten-minute routine for when I want to go deeper and a thirty-minute practice for when I'm feeling under the weather or at a big event. Find what works for you and then commit to doing it regularly.

● ●

Fail often

It's natural to fear failure. We want to protect ourselves from appearing foolish. We don't like others to see our weaknesses. But if we hold on to our fears, we simply can't grow. Making mistakes is how we learn. Failure is actually the basis of creation. If we don't know what wrong looks like, we'll never be able to recognise what's right. As an actor, I always felt my job was to make as many mistakes as possible, to push the boundaries and explore the limits of what was achievable in a given moment. Now, I encourage the people I work with to do the same. What's the worst that can happen? As far as I'm aware, no one has ever died because they made a mistake in a presentation or said the wrong thing in a meeting.

If you want to make an impact, you need to be prepared to fail often and learn quickly from your mistakes. That's how you hone your technique. You need to spend time reviewing your performance with a critical eye. Sometimes we try to protect ourselves and gloss over our mistakes, but if you want to find out what you're truly capable of, you need to be honest about your shortcomings. Make sure you factor review time into your diary each day and look for patterns. Don't beat yourself up – just notice what you're doing and look for opportunities to refine and make changes.

ACT OF COMMUNICATION
• •

REVIEW YOUR PERFORMANCE

The words 'performance' and 'review' drive fear into the hearts of many people. They tend to bring about an expectation of criticism and bad news, but I suggest viewing them with a sense of excitement and opportunity instead. Rather than waiting for someone to review you, regularly review yourself. Build time into your diary to reflect on your performance. When you put the phone down, give yourself a few moments to think about how you did and what you learned. Schedule fifteen-minute breaks between your meetings so that you have time to grab a pen and make some notes. At the very least, get into the habit of spending two minutes at the end of each day appraising your achievements. I suggest using the headings 'Strengths' and 'Stretches' to create a list of what you did well and what you want to work on going forward.

• •

Play

Technique is about bringing all the elements of IMPACT together. It's about making the tools your own and exploring your full range as a communicator. To that end, I encourage you to have fun and to play. The worst thing you can do as you develop your impact is to get stuck in your head. As soon as you start to rationalise, you get in your own way and inhibit your opportunity for growth. Instead, reserve judgement and look for possibilities. Play doesn't mean you have to be childish; you just need to remain open. When we play we suspend disbelief. We become receptive to other ways of seeing the world. It's a state you enter instantly when you see a great piece of theatre or watch a brilliant film. Rationally, you know the actors aren't really the characters they're pretending to be, and yet you follow the narrative and experience their emotions as if they were. Imagine what you could achieve if you gave yourself permission to play full out – to utilise the full range of your communication and really make an impact? Start to play with the tools we've explored and put the building blocks you need in place. Then take it one step at a time until you find your freedom and flow.

Chapter Seven

IN ACTION

Take centre stage

I hope you've found learning about the six ingredients of impact enlightening and thought-provoking. There's a lot to take in and many different tools to explore. Some things will make immediate sense and you'll be desperate to try them out. Others might take some time to understand and internalise. Whatever you do, don't wait to take action. Don't save the ideas in this book for later. Experiment with them now and make them your own.

You read this book because you want to develop and improve your communication in some way. Whether you want to be more persuasive on the phone, more influential in meetings or more inspiring when you present, the only way to get better is to put the tools and techniques into practice. If you want your ideas to be heard, you have to give them a voice. If you want to make the sale, you have to make the ask. If you want people to follow you, you have to allow yourself to be seen. You have to decide to act. You have to take centre stage.

Taking the spotlight can make you feel vulnerable, but if each ingredient of IMPACT is in place, you have nothing to worry about. Define your intention. Take control of your mindset. Expand your presence. Know your audience. Get clear on your content. And trust your technique. The IMPACT model is designed to keep you safe, whatever challenging situation you find yourself in. Use it as a pre-communication check-list and you'll know you're always ready to perform. Work your way through each ingredient and ensure that you have the necessary elements in place:

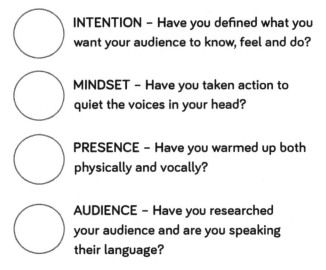

INTENTION – Have you defined what you want your audience to know, feel and do?

MINDSET – Have you taken action to quiet the voices in your head?

PRESENCE – Have you warmed up both physically and vocally?

AUDIENCE – Have you researched your audience and are you speaking their language?

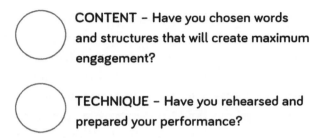

CONTENT – Have you chosen words and structures that will create maximum engagement?

TECHNIQUE – Have you rehearsed and prepared your performance?

If you can tick off each item above, you're ready to make an impact.

Get support

One of the biggest challenges with communication is that we can't see or hear what we're doing. Unless we employ a camera crew to follow us around 24/7, it's difficult to be objective about how we're coming across to others. We can't be both in the moment and watching from the sidelines. If you really want to improve, you need to get feedback. You need someone you trust to tell you what they see. Even the best actors need a director – someone who can help them tweak their performance and fully inhabit their role.

As you begin this journey to increase your impact, I suggest finding someone you trust to give you feedback. It could be a manager, a colleague or a coach. Look for someone who has the skill set and the qualities you want to develop and ask them to support you through the process. It's something worth investing in. Your skill as a communicator will determine your success in every area of your life. Every relationship you build, every pitch you win, every promotion you gain will, in some way, be down to the impact you make on your audience. It's a lifelong process of learning and improvement. Now that you understand how to develop your performance, don't underestimate the power at your fingertips. When you take control of your impact, you take control of your destiny. Find someone who can help you shine.

Make an impact

My final plea is that you share what you've learned in this book with others. The reason for this is twofold. Firstly, when you teach someone else what you've been working on, you embed the learning in yourself. The act of explaining the tools will deepen your knowledge and help you commit them to mental and physical memory. And secondly, I believe that the skills we've explored together in this book can make the world a better place. Everyone deserves to feel confident. Everyone deserves to be heard. Everyone deserves to be seen. So much of the conflict and pain that people experience in life is due to breakdowns in communication. If this book can change one conversation for the better, it was worth the effort of writing it.

So, here you stand at a fork in the road. You have the power to make a difference in your own life and the lives of those you interact with. You have the tools and the knowledge to be more confident and change the way you show up. You have the ability to increase your influence and the techniques to find the right words in any situation. The choice is yours. Do you want to stay in the shadows? Or do you want to step into the spotlight? It's time to make an impact.

Afterword

Thank you for reading this book. I hope that you've found the toolkit useful and that it has provoked you to think differently about the way you communicate. Most of all, I hope it has inspired you to take action and to change how you do things. If you would like to find out more about coaching, our public courses or running an IMPACT Masterclass or Accelerator Programme for your organisation, please visit www.inflow.global or email me at dominic@inflow.global.

I truly believe in the importance of the skills we teach, and it frustrates me that many people have to wait until adulthood to learn them. To help remedy this, at In Flow we're on a mission to support future generations of entrepreneurs and business leaders communicate with impact from the word go. If you know of a primary school in the UK that would benefit from one of our free workshops for children, please point them in our direction.

Finally, if you want to stay in touch and get regular tips on communication and performance, please sign up for our newsletter at www.inflow.global.

Good luck with your next performance, or, as we say in the world of acting, 'Break a leg'!

Further Reading

If you've been inspired to explore the topic of communication further, I highly recommend the following books and authors.

Anderson C (2016) TED Talks: The Official TED Guide to Public Speaking. London: Hodder & Stoughton.

Cialdini R B (2007) *Influence: The Psychology of Persuasion*. New York: Harper Business.

Covey S (1989) *The 7 Habits of Highly Effective People*. New York: Free Press.

Dale C and Peyton P (2019) *Physical Intelligence*. London: Simon & Schuster.

Goleman D (1996) *Emotional intelligence*. London: Bloomsbury.

Hagen U and Frankel H (2008) *Respect for Acting*. New York: Jossey Bass.

Hanh T N (2010) *You Are Here*. Boulder, CO: Shambhala Publications.

Heath C and Heath D (2008) *Made to Stick: Why Some Ideas Take Hold and Others Come Unstuck*. London: Arrow.

Johnstone K (2007) *Impro: Improvisation and the Theatre*. London: Methuen.

McCallion M (1999) *The Voice Book: For Everyone Who Wants to Make the Most of Their Voice* (2nd ed). London: Routledge.

Pink D H (2018) *To Sell Is Human*. Edinburgh: Canongate.

Acknowledgements

With any creative project, a huge amount of work goes on behind the scenes that the audience never sees. There are many people who have been part of this journey and who have helped me, directly and indirectly, to bring this book to life. I want to take a moment to thank them all publicly from the bottom of my heart.

My first and biggest thank you goes to my gorgeous wife, Laura. I couldn't have asked for a more supportive partner in life and in business. You've never complained as I've written into the small hours. You've listened supportively to my author's neurosis and reassured me that everything would be ok. You've read and reread my words whenever I've asked you to and given feedback that has transformed my writing for the better. All this while effortlessly juggling a million other things and never missing a beat. I am in awe. Thank you for being mine.

My second thank you is to my Nell. You'll never know the joy you brought me each time you came out to the office for a goodnight cuddle and sat on my knee watching me type. Your energy and love of life are a constant source of inspiration in everything I do.

To my family, thank you for always supporting me. Mum and Dad, you've taught me to believe that anything is possible if I set my mind to it. Abbie, Ben, Fran, Zoe, Nico, Eli, Max, Ada, Jane and Jamie, your love and encouragement means the world.

To my team at In Flow and all our amazing trainers, thank you for helping me to spread the word and create an impact. To the teams at RADA Business, Taming Tigers and Opposite Leg, thank you for introducing me to the world of training and for giving me the opportunity to grow my skills.

To Lucy, Joe and the team at Rethink Press, thank you for making this book a reality. Kathy and Rachel, your edits have made me sound intelligent and well educated. Katie, your cover makes me smile every time I look at it. I am also indebted to an amazing team of beta readers. Juliet Stott, Conrad Hornby, Katharine Harbord, Alexis Kingsbury and Katie Posner, your notes and constructive criticism helped me to raise my game. Matt Harbord, you went beyond the call of duty – thank you for being a true friend.

Thanks of course to all those who read the manuscript in advance and provided such lovely words of praise. It's especially humbling to see people I consider mentors lend their names to support my work. Ellis Jones, you taught me about the theatre. Steve Payne, you gave me the confidence to coach. Nick Walker, you trusted me at the beginning. Daniel Priestley, you made me believe I could write a book. Claire Dale, you championed me at every step along the way. I am deeply grateful to you all.

I would also like to recognise the amazing teachers who have shared their knowledge and wisdom with me over the years. Thanks, too, to all the brilliant actors and directors I have had the fortune to work with and learn my craft from. All of you have shaped and influenced the words I have written. In particular, I would like to say a special thank you to my childhood drama teachers, Erica Harley and Liz Manning, for sparking my curiosity about the art of acting, and to Annie Tyson and John Beschizza, who made my time at Drama Centre transformational.

Finally, I want to finish by thanking all of the clients and delegates who have trusted me to be their guide over the last ten years. You have taught me just as much as I have taught you, and your stories of success make all the hard work worthwhile.

Thank you all.

The Author

A specialist in communication and leadership, Dominic Colenso has been delivering training and one-to-one coaching in the private and public sectors for the last ten years.

Beginning his career as a professional actor, he worked extensively on stage and screen before training as a director at the Royal Academy of Dramatic Art in London. Performing in many of the UK's leading theatres, including the National Theatre and the Royal Court, Dominic has appeared on film in everything from BBC period dramas to big-budget action movies. He is best known for playing the role of Virgil Tracy in the Hollywood adaptation of *Thunderbirds*, with Bill Paxton and Sir Ben Kingsley.

Dominic's experience and fascination with how the body, breath and voice can influence performance led him to set up his communication skills training consultancy, In Flow, and to launch his career as a keynote speaker. Dominic and the In Flow team work with individuals and businesses around the world to help them speak and perform under pressure.

Find Dominic online at:

🌐 www.dominiccolenso.com and www.inflow.global

🐦 @dominiccolenso

💼 www.linkedin.com/in/dominiccolenso